Guerrillas and Terrorists

Guerrillas and Terrorists

RICHARD CLUTTERBUCK

FABER AND FABER LIMITED
3 Queen Square, London

First published in 1977
by Faber and Faber Limited
3 Queen Square London WC1
Printed in Great Britain
by Ebenezer Baylis and Son Ltd
The Trinity Press, Worcester, and London
All rights reserved

British Library Cataloguing in Publication Data

Clutterbuck, Richard
  Guerrillas and terrorists.
  1. Terrorism
  I. Title
  322.4'2   HV6431

  ISBN 0–571–11027–4

DEDICATED to the memory of
Professor G. S. R. KITSON CLARK

of Trinity College, Cambridge, who was my host
and companion throughout the 1975–76 Lees-
Knowles Lectures in what proved to be the last
weeks of his life. He has left us a lasting legacy from
his long life, both in his writings and in our memory
of him. It is consoling to record that he died as he
would have wished – reading a book in his room at
Trinity a few hours after dining in Hall.

Contents

1*

Preface

The theme of this book is that terrorism—the attack on an individual to frighten and coerce a large number of others—is as old as civilization itself. It is the recourse of a minority or even of a single dissident frustrated by the inability to make society shift in the desired direction by what that society regards as 'legitimate' means. It is primarily an attack on the rule of law, aimed either to destroy it or (as in more recent times) to change it radically to conform to the terrorist's own idea of society.

To protect itself from this coercion, and to protect its people's lives and possessions, a society needs an awareness of what the terrorists are trying to achieve, and a high degree of public co-operation with its policemen and soldiers. We need to understand how this kind of war is fought on both sides if we are to know how best to help those who are fighting, win it.

In this, the mass media play a vital role; they can both hinder and help but, providing that the police and the public understand what the press and television can do and co-operate with them, they are much more likely to help. In most countries, sadly, the media tell the people what the government wants them to be told, but in the relatively few remaining free societies it works the other way round; the media live by attracting viewers and readers and they can achieve this best by striking a chord with the section of the public for whom they cater. The overwhelming majority of the public detest political violence and terrorism and wish to help the police to defeat them. So, given the chance, the media will reflect this feeling. My purpose in writing this book is to contribute to the understanding and co-operation between the police, the public and the media.

This was the aim of the six Lees-Knowles Lectures which I gave at Cambridge University in 1975–76 and on which this book is based. I am immensely grateful to the Master of Trinity College, Cambridge, who administers the Lees-Knowles bequest and hosts these Lectures. Rather than bore my audience by pontificating on contemporary theory about violence and revolution, I tried to focus a beam of light in turn on some of the vital lessons to be learnt from conflicts which may have been obscured by excessive analysis—such as those in Vietnam, Malaya and Northern Ireland, and those involving Palestinian guerrillas inside and outside the Middle East. These cover both urban and rural guerrilla conflicts, and I also included an interlude on how the ability of organized bodies of soldiers to take care of themselves in remote parts of the world can be put to constructive use when they do not have to fight, in order to help remove some of the seeds of injustice and deprivation which might later lead to violence.

I hope that my beam of light will have picked out for the record some of the points worth remembering from these experiences and that these may help to illuminate what will, I think, remain the prevalent form of conflict for our time.

EXETER
December 1976   Richard Clutterbuck

1 Conflict for our time

'Kill one, frighten ten thousand.' *Old Chinese Proverb*

It is a strange anomaly that a government which will stand firm in the face of an ultimatum knowing that 10,000 of its citizens will die in the consequent invasion or bombardment, will give way in the face of a threat to the life of a single hostage. Individual violence is now more often used than invasion or bombardment as a means of international coercion, and is proving more effective than public demonstrations and riots for exerting internal pressure. Guerrillas and terrorists have existed for centuries, but it is only in the last few years that they have become a substantial force in international affairs and internal politics which it is vitally important for the people of the world to understand.

Guerrillas in the nineteenth century generally acted only as auxiliaries to regular armies, and terrorists who killed kings or archdukes seldom influenced government policy. Though kidnapping for ransom was not uncommon in the Middle Ages, it is only recently that it has become a major weapon for political blackmail and publicity. Guerrillas now exercise a power previously exercised only by governments. This can be done by half a dozen men or women, perhaps tacitly supported by governments, but more often acting independently or on behalf of a small group. They differ from the violent men commonly called criminals only in that the criminals act for personal material gain whereas terrorists act for wider political motives, though this may sometimes be a cloak for seeking personal power or fulfilment.

The strongest single factor which leads governments to give way to terrorists, internationally or internally, is television. This operates in several ways. It magnifies the actions of the terrorists, sometimes to the extent that publicity in itself may become their aim. The main reason, however, is that television brings their

13

violence on a personal level into the home of almost every citizen in the land in which they are operating, and in a good many others too.

Old style wars between armies do still occur, and can result in far heavier casualties than guerrilla operations. In the Indo-Pakistan War of 1971 and the Arab–Israeli War of 1973, more people were killed in a single day than the total number killed in five years of bitter fighting in Northern Ireland. Old style wars still attract old style popular fervour, despite the casualties, because people calling for war and governments launching invasions do not identify with 10,000 nameless casualties, any more than they identify with 10,000 flood or earthquake victims in some far country. On the other hand, because of television, we can and do identify with hostages, whose photographs we see in the press and whose tearful families talk to us from the screen in our own homes. It is all too easy to imagine those families being our own. There is a temptation to feel that the government should give whatever is necessary to get the hostages released and then find some way of sorting out the problem afterwards.

Governments can only stand firm in so far as they are able to carry public opinion with them. This may be difficult, especially if the country selected for the operation is one which has nothing to do with the dispute. This was one of the problems faced by Chancellor Kreisky in Austria in 1973 and again in 1975. Mr. Heath faced the same problem in 1970 when an aircraft containing, among others, twenty-one unaccompanied British school-children was held by Palestinian hi-jackers on Dawson's Field in Jordan. They were held as hostages for the release of another Palestinian terrorist, Leila Khaled, who had quite fortuitously fallen into British hands when an Israeli aircraft made an emergency landing at London Airport after her unsuccessful attempt to hi-jack it. If Mr. Heath had been uncompromising and had said that Leila Khaled would be handed over in custody to the Israelis, even if it meant twenty-one British children being blown up, it is unlikely that he would have carried the British public with him. The probable reaction would have been 'What do we care about Leila Khaled? To hell with the Arabs and the Israelis. Let them fight it out themselves. Get our kids home!' Leila Khaled was released. The British Government, however, refused to release her until all the hostages from all the countries involved had been released, and within a few months had stood completely firm in two other kidnappings—that of James Cross by the F.L.Q. (Front de Libération du Québec) in Canada and of Geoffrey Jackson by the Tupamaros in Uruguay. Their attitude proved to be strong enough to deter the selection of Britain for other international kidnapping operations during the next five years.

It is now evident that giving way in order to save the life of a hostage will probably do no more than postpone the issue and result in more hostages being placed in the same jeopardy later on. There are encouraging signs that governments are realizing this. In the autumn of 1975, the Irish Government, staunchly supported by the Dutch Government, stood firm for five nerve-wracking weeks while a Dutch industrialist, Dr. Herrema, was held at gunpoint by two I.R.A. terrorists. Even more commendable was the stout resistance of the Dutch Government in the face of two mass kidnappings by South Moluccan terrorists in Beilen and Amsterdam. Three of the victims in the hi-jacked train at Beilen were murdered, in one case brutally and publicly, the victim standing to be shot in full view in the open door of the train. Although no country can be wholly immune, the Republic of Ireland and Holland will now be at the hard rather than the soft end of the list of targets for operations by international terrorists.

By contrast, terrorists all over the world will have been encouraged to try again by the immediate capitulation of the Austrian Government when the OPEC ministers were kidnapped in Vienna in December 1975, and by the granting of sanctuary to the kidnappers by the Algerians. Austria must surely have gone to the very top of the list.

Rural guerrillas, though less in the news, also have a high record of success, other than in Latin America. This often passes unrecognized, because it merges imperceptibly into civil war or a link with a foreign invasion, as happened in China's own revolution in the late 1940s, and again in Vietnam and Cambodia. The effect of guerrilla operations may be such as to make it impossible for the government to resolve the country's problems or even to govern effectively at all. This is one of the aims. The result is that the grievances on which popular support for the guerrillas are based become worse. Where friendly countries have successfully assisted governments under attack by rural guerrillas, as in Malaysia and the Philippines, their military assistance has often been of less importance than their aid in supporting effective civil administration and helping the government to improve the lot of its people rather than to allow it to decline or relapse into chaos.

Guerrilla warfare and terrorism, rural or urban, internal or international, has undoubtedly now become the primary form of conflict for our time.

Internally, in many countries, there has been a disturbing dis-enchantment with constitutional methods amongst minorities which cannot get their own way. They find that direct action not only achieves results but also attracts publicity and builds up a fear amongst the public comparable to the fear induced in a crime-dominated community like Italy for organized criminal gangs. This fear would be the basis whereby they would subsequently impose their will on the majority if they were to overthrow the existing constitution. Such fear reached a peak in Northern Ireland, where in 1975 rival terrorist groups were competing. They generally turned their attacks away from the army onto the civil population and in 1975 more civilians were killed than in 1974 or 1973. Moreover, most of these were killed by clandestine assassination rather than by the indiscriminate bombing of previous years. No political party of any significance, and only a minute proportion of the population, supported either of these terrorist groups. Neither of them achieved results comparable with those of the Ulster Workers' Council, whose public utilities strike in 1974 overturned the Constitution and brought down the only government in which Protestants and Catholics had co-operated in the history of the Province. Yet the violence con-tinued, and by the end of that year 1 in 1,000 of the population had been killed and 1 in 100 wounded in the previous five years. The likeliest effect of such violence is not revolutionary change but a backlash which could do irreparable damage to the prospects for a peaceful society.

Rural guerrilla activity, though it attracts less publicity, has still continued in many parts of the world, mostly in under-developed countries, but also in some parts of Northern Ireland, especially South Armagh where in January 1976, for example, the murder of five Catholics in isolated farm houses by Protestant terrorists was followed by the murder of ten Protestants by the I.R.A. who stopped a mini-bus carrying men home from work on a country road. These killings were quite clearly aimed to terrorize the population of the opposing community.

A third aspect of this 'conflict for our time' is the external support of internal guerrilla and terrorist movements by sympathizers in foreign countries. These sympathizers may be members of fraternal revolutionary groups in other countries, or of communities which raise private funds or collect and smuggle weapons to the terrorists, as for example, a number of Irish American organizations do to the I.R.A.

Fourthly, support of this same kind may be given, openly or clandestinely, by foreign governments. This may sometimes be in support of resistance groups opposing foreign armies of occupation or colonial regimes. The Russian support of the M.P.L.A. in Angola during the Portuguese colonial era was an example of this. After Angola became independent, however, at least five foreign governments, including the Russians, were identified as supporting the three factions, M.P.L.A. (Movimiento Popular Libertação de Angola), F.N.L.A. (Frente Nacional Libertação de Angola), Unita (Uniao Nacional para a Independencia Total de Angola), in the subsequent civil war. Sometimes foreign governments calculatedly arouse and support internal conflicts as a means of weakening, coercing or even overthrowing the government in the target country. The Governments of Cuba and the United States have both been accused of doing this in a number of Latin American countries, and the Russian and Chinese Governments have done so in support of 'wars of national liberation' in newly independent African and Asian countries. The activities of the North Vietnamese Government in Thailand and of the Indian Government in supporting the Mukti Bahini in East Bengal in 1971 fall into the same category. In the latter case this activity was followed by an invasion by the Indian Army to establish the independent State of Bangladesh, but more often the support of internal conflicts has become a substitute for invasion by regular armies in the modern world.

A fifth version of 'conflict for our time' is direct action by international terrorist groups in countries in which they have no particular interest, but which are selected as a suitable stage for a spectacular hi-jacking or kidnapping for the purpose of exerting political blackmail on some quite different country, or simply to gain international publicity by 'armed propaganda'. The kidnapping of the OPEC oil ministers in Vienna in 1975 fell precisely into this category.

A sixth dimension of this conflict is the support by resident sympathizers in the country in which such international direct action is staged. This support may be given by immigrant or temporarily resident workers or students from the same country as the terrorists, such as Arab students in Germany providing facilities for Palestinian terrorists; alternatively, such facilities may be provided by indigenous Trotskyist or anarchist groups.

Thus, to recapitulate, six manifestations of this 'conflict for our time' may be detected, though they too could be further subdivided and often overlap: first, internal urban guerrilla activity; second, rural guerrilla activity; third, external support of either of these by sympathetic groups or communities in foreign countries; fourth, external support by foreign governments exploiting internal conflict, now replacing invasion as the commonest means of making war; fifth, direct action by international terrorist groups for international political blackmail or international publicity; and sixth, the support of such direct action by resident sympathizers in the country in which the action takes place.

These forms of conflict often arouse more intense emotion and bitterness than conventional forms of war. This is partly because a much larger percentage of the casualties are civilians, often individually unconcerned in the conflict, and includes a high proportion of women and children. Another reason is that the world has evolved no 'laws of war' or traditions of chivalry (such as, for example, the treatment of prisoners of war) in guerrilla or terrorist warfare. There is, therefore, something particularly horrifying about the plight of a defenceless hostage in the hands of kidnappers and something repugnant about a captured terrorist, even one who is guilty of torturing and killing his own victims, being tortured himself like a rat in a trap by his captors. Yet to understand and rid the world of such conflict it is particularly important to avoid judgements excessively clouded by emotion. One man's 'terrorist' is another man's 'freedom fighter'. Where the far Right see the hidden hand of world communism behind every guerrilla they dislike, or alternatively behind governments suppressing those guerrillas with whom they sympathize, the far Left see the C.I.A. in the same role.

Moral judgements are most commonly a rationalization of political judgements. I.R.A. members who are seen as 'bad guys' by the majority of Southern Irishmen, may be seen as 'good guys' by the majority of Irish Americans. The Pakistanis bitterly regarded the Indian support of the Mukti Bahini as a cynical prelude to invasion, while the Indians regarded it as legitimate support of a liberation movement by Bengalis who had already overwhelmingly expressed their desire for independence at the polls. What seem 'bad guys' to Brazilians, Chileans or South Africans may seem 'good guys' to millions in other countries who sympathize with their resort to violence in default of any other means of achieving what they see as legitimate aims. Resistance fighters against the German occupation of France in the Second World War, who used clandestine methods of killing which the Germans treated as terrorism, were regarded by both the French and British as heroes.

Guerrilla warfare may be regarded as legitimate where it is against a government which the majority of the population regard as illegitimate—such as a government installed by foreign occupation (e.g. the Vichy Government in France), a colonial government or a minority government inheriting power from a colonial government (as in South Africa or Rhodesia). It is not so easy to judge the legitimacy of a government installed by an internal *coup d'état* or by a revolution, which invariably claims that it has the support of the people while its opponents invariably declare that it has not.

There is also an element of value judgement in assessing the morality of guerrilla warfare against a government which, though legitimately elected by a majority, denies equal rights or fair treatment to a minority in its own country. Many Catholics in Northern Ireland would claim that this has been their fate for the past fifty years, and that there has been no effective constitutional means of securing fair treatment.

Even more difficult is the moral judgement involved in deciding whether a part of a country has a right to secede. Had Norway the right to secede from Sweden in 1905, or had the Swedes the right to keep them in Sweden by force? Did the Southern states of America have the right to secede from the Union in 1861 if the majority of their people wished it? (and did they wish it?) Has Canada a right to be independent from the United States? Have the Protestant majority in the six Northern counties of Ireland a right to be independent from Ireland as a whole, in which the majority would be Catholic? Some people would answer yes to one question and no to another in which the criteria were virtually identical.

Whether guerrilla warfare is judged to be legitimate or not, it almost inevitably incorporates an element of terrorism. This is because the government in the country will invariably regard it as illegitimate and will treat those members of the population who support the guerrillas as criminals. Thus, whatever the true sympathies of the majority of the population, the proportion prepared to take the risk of supporting the guerrillas will usually only be a small minority so, to survive at all, the guerrillas will have to put the population at large in sufficient fear to induce an adequate proportion to support them and to deter the remainder from supporting the government—in other words, to impose an element of terror.

Terrorism may, however, be used by groups which could not possibly claim to be conducting a guerrilla campaign and which have no appreciable support at all amongst the population of the country in which they are operating—whether it is their own country or another. Examples were the Symbionese Liberation Army in the U.S.A., the Angry Brigade in Britain, the Red Army Fraction in West Germany and the United Red Army in Japan. Such movements are almost wholly intellectual and see no immediate prospect of attracting even a minority mass base. Their purpose is not always easy to detect. It may be simply to remain in existence as a propaganda cell for the general purpose of discrediting the existing regime, but without a specific alternative in mind; it may be to provoke the government to over-react and thereby lose popularity; or it may simply be to satisfy an angry, destructive urge arising from individual frustration. In any of these cases it may find itself joining forces with the criminal world for mutual benefit—the criminal gangs finding it useful to confuse the police by operating behind a political cover, and the political groups making use of the professional services of the criminals. Both also gain materially from the increased opportunity to extort ransom money, so that the tendency of such partnerships is to slide wholly into the criminal world.

Terrorism is not precisely the same as violence. Terrorism aims, by the use of violence or the threat of violence, to coerce governments, authorities or populations by inducing fear. Television has enormously expanded their ability to do so. In the television age, the Chinese proverb quoted at the head of this chapter might be amended to read: 'Kill one, frighten ten million'.

2 Rooted in history

When did guerrilla warfare and terrorism begin? Fashionable though they are, they are certainly not new. Examples are quoted by the earliest historians, such as Herodotus, and by the earliest philosophers of war, such as Sun Tzu. It is a reasonable conjecture, however, that they are a good deal older than that, and almost certainly the oldest form of war, dating from the dawn of civilization.

Man emerged from the forest about one and a half million years ago. Till then he had lived, like the other apes, by plucking nuts and fruits from the trees. Outside in the open plain, life was tougher. Short of nuts and fruit, he developed a taste for meat. In competing with the other animals both for vegetable and animal food, however, he suffered serious disadvantages. Most of them could run much faster than he could and the carnivorous animals had superior teeth and claws designed to kill, which he did not. He only survived because of his superior intelligence. He learned to throw missiles to kill at a distance, and later to fashion them into weapons which could kill still better. He also learned to co-operate.

Through ninety-nine per cent of the ages during which man has been an omnivorous animal, that was how he lived, gradually developing the power to co-operate in the form of hunting groups and later tribes. It was only 10,000 years ago that he learned to cultivate and to apply his skill with tools to tilling the ground and not merely to killing other animals. Some time between those dates, between a million and ten thousand years ago, he must have begun to develop the idea of a rule of law to make the community—the hunting group and the tribe—more efficient. This rule of law will clearly have become more important still when the members of the community began to cultivate seeds which took months to bear fruit, and to keep domestic animals.

A rule of law requires someone to enforce it, and later, a hierarchy of chiefs who, by common consent or by *force majeure*, punish on behalf of the community the dissidents who break its laws. There can be no doubt that, as soon as such chiefs began to operate, there were dissidents who challenged their authority. They will soon have discovered that the chief was, as an individual, just as vulnerable to weapons as the animals who were killed for food.

As the community developed, the chiefs required agents to organize activities and enforce the law. These agents themselves became outposts of authority just as vulnerable as the chiefs themselves. Over the centuries, the weapon of the dissident developed from the rock, to the spear, to the knife. At the same time communities would fight each other, fostering further weapon development, leading on to the gun and the bomb of the last 500 years.

Despite their vastly greater lethal capacity, men generally do less killing than other animals, except when they indulge in the mass lunacy of war. Within communities themselves the surprising thing is that there seems always to have been very little killing. One reason for this is that the chiefs and their agents, stimulated by the need for defence against other communities, have organized armed forces which can also be used for internal security and have been able to stifle any attempt by dissidents to organize forces powerful enough to challenge them. This has no doubt been resented through the ages, and still is resented, by those who believe that man should be wholly and individually free, that civilization is a form of violence, and that 'the Queen's peace' is itself a product of State terror.

Most people, however, *want* civilization and have regarded it as beneficial since the day it began. They wanted to reap what they had sown; to find their cave or home intact, their wife unraped and their children not carted off into slavery while they were out hunting; not to live under the constant threat of violent death as the wild animals did; and to share the fruits of co-operative endeavour.

Most of those who today wish to overthrow constitutional government by force or to change society by terror, even if they do so in the name of nationalism, are usually motivated by the philosophy of the anarchist or the Marxist—or of the Marxist's close totalitarian cousin, the fascist. The anarchist, by definition, wants no hierarchy—he wants to take man back to the freedom of the animals in the jungle. The Marxist goes to the other extreme. He wishes to develop civilization to the level achieved by the ants where organization is total and conformity is accepted without question and enforced by most members of the community upon others. The organization and instincts of the ants are so developed that dissent is rare and when it occurs the majority snuff it out forcibly without waiting for orders. In a pure Marxist society this particular instinct, which has taken millions of years to develop in the ants, would be inculcated by an indoctrination of children from the cradle—and this is where the Marxist and the fascist become indistinguishable. Such instincts, however, do not come naturally to men, who do not want either the wild freedom of the jungle or the total order of the ant-hill. That is why the anarchist can never achieve his aim without force and why Lenin recorded, rightly, that 'no dictatorship of the proletariat is to be thought of without terror and violence'.

By the time that history began to be recorded, about 2,500 years ago, two separate kinds of guerrilla warfare had begun to emerge. First was the development of organized revolt against established government—of which the rising of the slaves led by Spartacus in Rome, 2,000 years ago, is typical. Second was the resistance to foreign occupation or domination by a tribe or community subdued by another, as typified by the resistance of the Scythians to Persian occupation in 512 B.C.

These two kinds of resistance are discernible throughout history, throughout the centuries of the Roman Empire, the operations of Hannibal, and the repeated invasions and subjugations of one people by another—the Goths, the Huns, the Vikings and the Normans. Guerrilla operations were sometimes complementary to the formal operations of armies. The question as to whether the resistance was against indigenous government or against foreign occupation was often arguable: the English no doubt regarded the Scottish and Welsh guerrillas as rebellious subjects, while the Scots and Welsh regarded the English as foreign invaders; the Irish have been resisting English occupation since the eleventh century. Certainly, up till the end of the seventeenth century, reaction to such resistance was ruthless. The only variation in punishment would be whether death was or was not preceded by torture. Might was right.

In the eighteenth century, along with the Enlightenment, this rigid attitude began, almost imperceptibly, to crack. Governments began to realize that over-reaction by their agents could be counter-productive. In 1737 Captain Porteous, commanding a British Army detachment in Edinburgh, opened fire on rioting Scots and seventeen were killed or wounded. He was charged with murder, convicted and sentenced to death. While he was awaiting the hearing of his appeal, the Scots spoiled the effect by breaking into the prison and lynching him, but the event was a significant one. In the subsequent two and a half centuries, other soldiers and policemen were to be charged and convicted for over-reacting. This was because governments were learning that the most important battle in guerrilla warfare was the battle for the support of the people. As Mao Tse-Tung put it, the guerrilla is the fish and the people are the sea. If the sea provides a friendly environment the guerrilla will survive, and if that environment is hostile to the soldier he will drown.

Mao Tse-Tung's excellent analogy is, however, misleading in one respect. It is quite unnecessary for *all* the people to be friendly or *all* to be hostile. In practice, there is invariably a mixture, and a large proportion of the people, usually a majority, have no wish to get involved and will conform to the dictates of either side if expressed by a man with a gun. Probably a fair average is that only about one per cent of people feel strongly enough to wish to risk their own lives in support of either the guerrillas or the government, another ten per cent may have sufficient preference to follow the lead of the activists on either side, while as many as eighty per cent do their utmost to keep themselves and their families out of the battle. The art of the soldier is to reduce the number who are willing to give active support to the guerrilla to the extent that he can no longer survive, while at the same time encouraging enough of the remainder to give the information the soldier needs to find and eliminate his foe. The art of the guerrilla is much the same in reverse—to retain enough support to be able to operate, and to handle things in such a way that the remainder become disenchanted with the

government, withhold such information, and hamper and de-
moralize the soldiers and other agents of the government.

What constitutes a 'friendly sea' for the guerrilla? This may
vary. If he is based in dense jungle, emerging only to carry out
raids, the jungle is friendly in that it is hard for the soldiers to find
him, but he must still rely on a proportion of the population outside the jungle being prepared to take risks to provide him with
food and other supplies. If, as is more common, the guerrilla has
to live clandestinely amongst the local population, either in town
or country, then a higher proportion of the people need to be
involved in his support if he is to survive. There must be an
adequate number of 'safe houses' in which he can be sure of taking
refuge in emergency, and these must be in neighbourhoods where
public opinion as a whole is at least not hostile, so that neither he
nor those who give him refuge will be reported to the government
authorities. In some areas this may be so because the people are
racially or in some other way closely linked with the guerrillas and
their cause. In other areas this alone may not be enough and a
degree of terror will be needed to deter people from reporting
what they see.

There was an element of both these factors during the American
War of Independence in 1775–83. In Massachusetts sentiment ran
strongly against the Redcoats. A large proportion of householders
in farms and country towns in 1775 were members of the militia
and had weapons in their houses, with the approval of the Colonial
Government, as it was essential for isolated communities to be
able to stand to arms at short notice in order to defend themselves
against the Indians or, until a few years previously, against rival
French colonists from Canada. A number were selected to be at
instant readiness as 'Minutemen'. They had had plenty of
experience of this over the years, and were far more efficient as
fighting soldiers than the Redcoats, as it was about fifteen years
since the British had been involved in a major war. Thus, when
they took to the lanes and hedgerows to harass the column of
Redcoats marching through Lexington to Concord and back, they
were not only superior in musketry and field craft, but they could
also knock on the door of almost any house in the certainty that
they would be given food or sanctuary. It thus became virtually
impossible for the British Army to operate outside the city of

Boston except in large armed bodies in tactical formation, and these too were very vulnerable.

In the American colonies as a whole, however, most historians agree that, at the most, one third of the people supported the rebellion. Another third wished to remain British, and the remainder, as always, didn't mind so much who won so long as they did not get involved and could go on farming or trading in peace. The skill of the guerrilla leaders, like Francis Marion, was to know where they could operate without being given away, and where they could safely turn for shelter or supplies. All the same, particularly in the South, a good deal of terror was necessary. Initially, the British, under General Sir Henry Clinton, followed an enlightened policy to attract people to the willing support of 'law and order' with considerable success; he encouraged rebel soldiers to defect by a generous system of granting parole on an undertaking that they would not take up arms against the British. By the summer of 1780, the rebellion in the Southern states seemed to be over, and Clinton handed over responsibility to his subordinate, Lord Cornwallis, and moved his headquarters to New York. Cornwallis, though an able general, was unable or unwilling to follow this policy. Guerrilla movements grew, and so did support for them. Guerrilla actions provoked reprisals, which further increased this support. Within a year the situation was totally transformed, and Cornwallis moved northwards, harassed both by regular American forces and by the guerrillas, to be besieged and defeated at Yorktown.

This pattern of guerrilla forces acting in conjunction with regular forces predominated throughout the nineteenth century and until the middle of the twentieth. Napoleon himself came to realize that what led to his downfall was his decision to get involved in Spain in 1808. The Spaniards made ruthless guer-rillas, as they and their blood descendants in Latin America have repeatedly proved ever since. During 1808 to 1814 they, like the men of Lexington and Concord, could rely on shelter and susten-ance almost anywhere. In addition, they had access to the more secure sanctuary of the encampments of Wellington's armies, in winter behind the lines of Torres Vedras and in summer wherever he campaigned in conjunction with them. Napoleon—like Hitler 130 years later in Greece and Yugoslavia—had to deploy vast numbers of troops to Spain from his major theatre of war on the Eastern Front. And on that Front itself Russian guerrillas played a decisive part in the destruction of the Grand Army in its retreat from Moscow in 1812.

Though writers from the early nineteenth century onwards began to underline the political significance of guerrilla war, independent guerrilla action remained rare. The revolutionary stage was set on the barricades and in the public squares, rather than in the back streets or the forests. Engels had little confidence in the success of either in Europe, commenting sadly in 1870 that fanaticism and national enthusiasm were not customary amongst civilized nations, but only amongst barbarians. He admired the resistance of the Algerians against the French and the Chinese against their own Manchu rulers. Marx shared his view, and saw no hope for the guerrillas or the men on the barricades unless they were joined by at least part of the regular army.

While independent guerrilla operations in Europe were rare, one of the biggest in history occurred in China in the middle of the nineteenth century. In 1847, Hung Hsiu-Chuan led the revolt of the 'Long Hair Rebels'. His manifesto, based on an extreme interpretation of Christianity, bore some remarkable similarities to the religion of Mao Tse-Tung. It demanded total State ownership, and allegiance to a single religion. His army, consisting initially of a few thousand peasants based in a remote area of Eastern Kwangsi, built up its popularity by attacking tax collectors while strictly respecting the rights of the local population. Like Mao Tse-Tung's army in Yenan in the following century, Hung's army grew and was gradually converted into an orthodox army, advancing down the Yangtze to Nanking and then to Tientsin. Hereafter, the erstwhile guerrillas fell prey to the temptations of a good life, and began to lose both their effectiveness and their popularity. Learning from Hung's earlier successes, a number of the Emperor's army commanders began to take care that their troops treated the local population with consideration, and Hung's fortunes declined. The final defeat of the rebels, however, was completed with extreme ruthlessness, and it is estimated that twenty million people in all were killed. This over-reaction was probably a major factor in the eventual overthrow of the Manchu dynasty.

Another war in which guerrillas operated more in their own right than in conjunction with a regular army was the South African War in 1899–1901. Initially the Boers, who had a numerical superiority of about two to one, tried to operate as a regular army but, despite some early victories, they failed because they were playing the British Regular Army at its own game. Within a few months the British had been substantially reinforced and the Boers wisely changed their organization and their tactics to operate largely as small mobile guerrilla commandos. It took the British two more years to subdue them, and even this was largely due to the experience of the later British commanders, like Lord Kitchener, with Imperial Policing and war in the wide open spaces.

Though it occurred in a major war, the revolt organized by T. E. Lawrence in Arabia in 1916–17 was initially a guerrilla war in its own right, though at the very end it began to link up with Allenby's armies marching from Jerusalem to Damascus. To begin with, Lawrence's aim was to make it impossible for the Turkish garrison of 100,000 men at Medina to survive at the end of a 700-mile railway across the desert from Damascus. He realized that the last thing to do was to launch the enthusiastic but ill-equipped and loosely organized Arabs at either the main Turkish garrisons or even the small defensive posts along the railway. Much more effective would be for small columns to blow up the railway repeatedly and slip away into the desert, so that the Turks would be constantly chasing an enemy they never saw. Only once, and late in the campaign, did the Arabs make a major attack, and that was to capture the port of Akaba, in which they achieved total surprise by attacking from the desert side. The Turks did not even know they were there and were standing by to repel an attack from the sea. Otherwise, the guerrillas actually fought the soldiers as seldom as they could. A more recent writer, Robert Taber, described this as the 'War of the Flea'.

Lawrence also had the shrewd military judgement to realize that, in the broader situation of the war, it would be a mistake to force the Turks to withdraw their 100,000 men from Medina. It would be better to keep them there, dependent on their single-line railway, but unable to withdraw down it, so that they would gradually bleed to death. He described the guerrillas as '. . . an influence . . . intangible . . . a vapour . . .' By contrast regular armies were 'like plants . . . firm rooted, nourished through long stems to the head'. Ultimately, the vapour would cause the plant to over-extend itself, wither and die.

Many of the lessons learned from Lawrence were applied in the resistance movements against German and Japanese occupation in the Second World War. These movements themselves were often fragmented, usually between communist and nationalist groups, which often fought each other as bitterly as they fought the Germans. Almost everywhere, however, the communist leadership emerged triumphant, with immensely enhanced experience, not only of guerrilla tactics, but also of the clandestine organization of popular support.

So long as the Germans were in occupation, they could rely, like the Minutemen in Massachusetts and the Spaniards in the Peninsular War, on shelter and supplies from the local population —as fish in a friendly sea. After the war, however, when fighting in some cases continued between communists and nationalists, the people usually preferred the prospect of a national government to that of a communist government which, apart from its ideology, they thought would probably not be wholly independent of Moscow. The communist guerrillas therefore required a sanctuary outside the country, in which to rest, train and re-equip. In Greece, such a sanctuary was provided by Yugoslavia until Tito broke with Moscow in 1948 and the sanctuary was thereafter denied. The Greek communist guerrillas thereafter quickly collapsed.

During the Second World War, and before it, one of the greatest practitioners of guerrilla warfare, and, with Lawrence, one of its most lucid philosophers, was fighting and winning what was probably the greatest guerrilla war in history, in China. Mao Tse-Tung's guerrilla philosophy, lucid as it is, has unfortunately been blurred by the fact that his campaign was a three-cornered one. For most of it, the Japanese were in partial occupation of his country, and he was fighting not only the Japanese, but the then legitimate government of China, the Kuomintang—who were themselves also resisting the Japanese. After the Japanese were defeated by the Allies in 1945 and withdrew from China, the war became a civil war, like Hung's war a century earlier. Nevertheless, because so much of it is written down, Mao's philosophy is there to be studied for those who wish to do so.

Reference has already been made to his analogy of the guerrilla being a fish in the sea of the population. Like Hung, Mao always stressed the importance of meticulous respect for the lives and property of the local population. This not only paid dividends in the war, but it also meant that for half a century after he began his rebellion and a quarter of a century after he completed it, he enjoyed a degree of respect and affection from his people which probably exceeded that of any other leader in the world.

Mao Tse-Tung laid down three phases for development of a revolutionary campaign—the organization phase, the guerrilla phase and the phase of mobile war. In the organization phase, it was necessary to build up not only local guerrilla forces in the villages, but also a structure of 'cadres' to organize their support by the population. For this purpose, 'agit-prop' teams toured the villages, drawing the attention of the peasants to the ways in which they were being denied the fruits of their labour, and explaining to them what they could do about it. At the same time, the guerrillas were to carry out 'selective terror' against government officials so that they would either turn a blind eye to the guerrillas' activities, or be eliminated. In order to gain popularity selective terror was also used to eliminate landlords and others whom the people disliked. It was also used to deter informers, thereby denying the government the services of that percentage from which it would normally expect support.

This gradually led into phase two, the guerrilla phase. Selective assassinations continued, but were supplemented by guerrilla attacks on isolated army posts, ambushes of troops moving along the roads (primarily to acquire their weapons) and the blowing up of roads and railways. By these means it was made more and more difficult for the government to maintain its isolated administrative posts and officials, and eventually even to maintain a military presence. It was then possible to extend revolutionary government until districts, and then regions, and eventually whole provinces, were free of government control. In these 'liberated areas' it was possible for the guerrillas to be reorganized (again like Hung's guerrillas) into battalions and divisions in readiness for the third phase.

Phase three was mobile war—which really amounted to civil war. The revolutionary armies fought the government forces, driving them further and further back towards the major cities, until eventually the cities were encircled by a hostile countryside and fell like ripe plums.

This philosophy was put into practice by Vo Nguyen Giap against the French in Indo-China in 1947–54 and, because the country was smaller, and there was no third power involved, the shape of Giap's campaign was easier to discern. This will be examined in the next chapter.

Another historical development of the twentieth century has been that of the urban guerrilla. Though there have always been individual assassinations, the first recorded example of a guerrilla leader acting in an urban environment with a tactical plan to achieve a political aim was probably that of Michael Collins in Ireland in 1919–20. His war was totally different from the fighting on the barricades in Europe in the nineteenth century, and from the taking over of army units, depots, factories, ships, railways and telephone exchanges by the Bolsheviks in Russia in 1917. Collins' example was later followed by the Irgun Zvai Leumi in Palestine in 1945–48. Thereafter, it was largely in abeyance until 1967, when urban terrorism began to develop in Latin America, and later in the rest of the world. This, too, will be the subject of a later chapter. Meanwhile, rural guerrilla activity still continues in parts of Asia and Africa, and rather less successfully in Latin America, and remains the principal method by which China would resist an invasion by Russia, were it ever to occur. It is therefore worth looking at some of the lessons learnt from the successful and unsuccessful rural guerrilla campaigns in South East Asia since 1945.

3   Lessons from South East Asia

So much has been written about South East Asia in the past ten years that the lessons applicable to guerrilla warfare have become obscured. One reason for this was that, after 1965, the war in Vietnam ceased to be primarily a guerrilla war at all—that is, guerrilla warfare became no more than complementary to conventional warfare between large armies, as in the nineteenth century. From 1965 to 1970, ninety per cent of those fighting against the government were in North Vietnamese regular army divisions and were opposed by regular divisions of the South Vietnamese and U.S. Armies. By 1972, the U.S. regular divisions had left and the war was between the North Vietnamese and South Vietnamese regular armies, the North Vietnamese advancing in Second World War style with tanks and artillery in their unsuccessful invasion of 1972, and their successful invasion of 1975. This would be defined as 'limited war' by those who regarded North and South Vietnam as independent countries, or 'civil war' by those who regarded Vietnam all the time as a single country. It could be described as the 'mobile war' phase of Mao Tse-Tung's strategy, which had superseded the guerrilla phase in 1965. Guerrilla warfare did continue in Laos and Cambodia, and is still continuing on a very small scale in Thailand and Malaysia, but nearly all the books have been about Vietnam.

This is a pity, because the years 1945–65 saw the most important developments in the history of Mao Tse-Tung's rural pattern of guerrilla warfare, and of the techniques for opposing it. It had some classic successes, notably by General Giap against the French from 1946 to 1954, and against the American-supported South Vietnamese from 1959 to 1964; also some classic failures, as in the Philippines from 1950 to 1953, and in Malaya from 1948 to 1960.

2

The Vietminh campaign against the French in Indo-China from 1946 to 1954 may well remain in the history books for all time as the finest example of Mao Tse-Tung's strategy in action. Ho Chi Minh and his guerrilla commander Vo Nguyen Giap in fact attempted a Leninist-style revolution first, in the cities of Hanoi and Haiphong, with strikes and mass demonstrations on the streets supplemented by bombs and assassinations. This was nothing unusual. The Chinese communists had also tried it unsuccessfully in Shanghai in the 1920s, and it was the young Mao Tse-Tung's interpretation of this failure which led him to the 'heretical' conclusion that a peasant-based revolution had more chance of success in China. This does not alter the fact that the Leninist urban revolution in the streets and factories (not to be confused with urban terrorism which plays only a small part in it) is still the quickest method, and the Vietminh were probably wise to attempt it first before resorting to Mao Tse-Tung's 'protracted war' in the countryside.

The two strategies are in fact the reverse of each other. In the urban strategy the revolutionaries seize the centres of government and industry and then the arteries of communication—railways and telecommunications—so that the government outposts, denied sustenance through root and branch, wither on the vine. In the rural strategy the revolutionaries work in from the twigs down the branches until the trunk and roots die from lack of sustenance from the foliage. Either strategy can be successful, though the environment—the relative importance of town and country to the economy, the state of communications, the distances, the terrain, the attitude of the public and availability of secure bases—may give one strategy a better chance than the other.

Having failed in Hanoi and Haiphong, the Vietminh took to the jungle late in 1946. They were already well prepared for pro-tracted war, because the 'organization phase' had been in progress for over two years, starting during the Japanese occupation in 1944. Ho and Giap had begun from the bottom, recruiting tiny bands of guerrillas and tiny cells of cadres in the remote areas into which the over-extended Japanese occupation forces did not attempt to penetrate. Agit-prop teams from these villages then toured other villages recruiting further guerrilla bands and cells. By the time of the Japanese defeat in August 1945, Ho Chi Minh had already built up a network of control in a large part of the country, and he attempted to negotiate with the Americans for recognition as the legitimate government. The Americans were initially sympathetic because they had no wish to see French colonialism restored, but were frustrated by the implacable opposition of General De Gaulle, whom they felt they had to carry with them as one of the 'Big Five' in their planned post-war order for the world. The French colonists were therefore re-established and Ho Chi Minh attempted to negotiate with them too, backed by the violence on the streets, before deciding to fall back on his well established infrastructure in the countryside.

From 1946 to 1949 the Vietminh extended this infra-structure and then began to build up their guerrilla activity, merging into phase two of the Mao Tse-Tung strategy. French administrators and their Indo-Chinese officials and collaborators were assassinated, military outposts raided and vehicles ambushed on the road. The Vietminh made progress, but so did the French, and it is hard to say which way that phase of the war would have gone, but for the decisive change brought about by the completion of the occupation of China by Mao Tse-Tung's People's Liberation Army in October 1949.

From 1950 onwards, the Vietminh had what Bernard Fall described as an 'active sanctuary' beyond the long border with China. They therefore judged that they need no longer wait for the consolidation of 'liberated areas' within Indo-China before starting to reorganize and train their guerrilla units for the mobile war of phase three. They made the first beginnings of merging into phase three when the Vietminh units crossed the frontier and captured three French frontier forts.

Encouraged by this success, Giap made one of his rare strategic errors. He tried to escalate the war in 1951–52 by sending strong mobile columns from the Chinese border deep into Vietnam to fight and attempt to destroy the French Army. This was premature, and they were defeated.

In 1952–53, Giap abandoned phase three and continued the steady progress of his guerrilla war. Plagued by raids and ambushes, the French gradually concentrated their forces and their administrators—both French and Indo-Chinese—into the fertile Red River delta, with Hanoi near the head of it. Eventually, all of them, including their families, were confined, especially at night, in a rash of fortified camps spread about the delta. During the day, armed columns moved between these fortresses, and airborne forces made forays deep into Laos and elsewhere. In the south of Vietnam and Cambodia French administration continued reasonably uninterrupted, but in the north, the Vietminh writ prevailed everywhere except in the cities of Hanoi and Haiphong and the fortified French camps.

By 1954, even powerful French armoured columns in regimental strength were being ambushed and destroyed by Giap's strong guerrilla forces. This period of the war has been superbly recorded for history in Bernard Fall's *Street Without Joy* (London, Pall Mall Press 1964). For the second time, the transition into phase three can be said to have started.

It was now the turn of the French to make their blunder. Encouraged by their success in 1951–52, they were convinced that they could win the pitched battles of the mobile war. They therefore decided to lure Giap's forces into such a pitched battle and destroy them. Using their air superiority, they established a very strong fortified base on the north-western border between Vietnam and Laos at Dien Bien Phu. From here, they patrolled in the hope of rallying loyalist supporters who feared that a Vietminh victory would result in domination by the Chinese. The French judged that Giap would concentrate his forces to attack Dien Bien Phu, where they would decisively defeat him.

The French had underestimated Giap's determination and tactical skill. Giap realized that it would be the French artillery and air support which would decide the battle; also that the French base was utterly dependent on air supply. The answer to both of these was to bring up his own artillery—which the French had judged to be impossible.

Confident that the 'sea' around Dien Bien Phu was friendly, and making use of the unlimited manpower available to him, Giap man-handled heavy guns along the mountainous trails from China. It was an episode of which Hannibal would have been proud. Giap used his artillery to destroy the French artillery and then to shell the air-strip so that the French were unable to maintain their supplies. The siege lasted for five and a half months, but the end was inevitable. Giap's military victory was complete, and the French withdrew from Vietnam.

During the same period—1948 to 1954—two other communist guerrilla movements had been attempting to follow Mao Tse-Tung's strategy—in the Philippines and in Malaya. In both cases the backs of their rebellions had broken by 1953, before the fall of Dien Bien Phu. In the Philippines, the main reason for this was the enlightened application by Magsaysay, first as Defence Minister and then as President, of Mao Tse-Tung's own precept of making the sea friendly for the fish. By land reform coupled with adequate security to protect those who co-operated with the government, Magsaysay convinced the population that life under his government would be better than life under the communists, and it was the guerrillas who drowned in an unfriendly sea. In Malaya, though the back of the rebellion was broken by 1953, it continued for seven more years before the guerrillas were finally beaten, during which time a great deal was learned about their detailed organization, and a great deal of progress was made in the art of counter-guerrilla warfare.

During the decisive part of the campaign, Malaya was a British colony. In 1955 it became self-governing, and was fully independent for the last three years of the campaign from 1957 to 1960, though, at the request of the Malayan Government, British troops continued to operate alongside Malayan troops and police, under a British General as Director of Operations responsible to the Malayan Government.

Like their comrades in Indo-China, the Malayan communists had built up a strong guerrilla force and infrastructure during 1943 to 1945, based on the rural areas into which the Japanese did not have enough troops to penetrate. The British gave active support to this resistance movement, sending in an advisory team under John Davis, who became a trusted personal friend of one of the guerrilla leaders, Chin Peng, who was later to become the leader of the rebellion against the British.

The Malayan Communist Party (M.C.P.) organization was based almost exclusively on the Chinese element in the Malayan population, of which the racial mixture was 49 per cent Malay, 39 per cent Chinese and 12 per cent Indian. The Malays never supported the M.C.P., which was itself almost exclusively Chinese, because they feared that if it came to power they would lose control of their own country to an immigrant race.

During 1943 to 1945, the main M.C.P. cadre organization was built up in predominantly Chinese areas in the north and south of the country, in the States of Perak and Johore. Villages which became bywords for resistance during the Japanese occupation—such as Sungei Siput, Chemor, Yong Peng and Kulai—reappeared as the hard core in the Emergency of 1948–60, and many of them are back in the news again with the guerrilla activity which has revived since 1967.

When the Second World War ended in 1945 the M.C.P., like the Vietminh, first attempted an urban revolution on the Leninist pattern, with strikes and riots and intimidation, but by 1948 this was clearly failing to attract the support of the commercially-minded Chinese in the cities. Chin Peng had by now become Secretary General of the M.C.P. and, like Ho Chi Minh, he decided to take to the jungle.

Many wartime guerrilla camps had been kept in readiness, together with stocks of buried weapons. Eight regiments of guerrillas were ready to remobilize, their names having been kept recorded in a well-organized Old Comrades Association. The cadres were also very much alive, particularly in the Chinese 'squatter' communities on the fringe of the jungle. These squatters had moved there to escape the attention of the Japanese in the villages and had taken over tracts of abandoned rubber estates which they cultivated for food. Being on the edge of the jungle, and far from any road, these squatter settlements proved ideal for supplying the guerrilla units both during the Japanese occupation and when they remobilized in 1948.

The initial successes of the guerrillas were such that the Government realized that it was essential to move these squatters into villages, where they could be prevented from smuggling food, and protected from reprisals if they did not wish to do so. Though many of them certainly did sympathize with the guerrillas, the majority had had their fill of conflict and were anxious to get back to a more secure and prosperous way of life, in which they could better provide for their children. There was surprisingly little resistance to the resettlement of some 400,000 squatters into 410 New Villages during eighteen months in 1950–51.

This resettlement was carried out by a wise Director of Operations, Lieutenant-General Sir Harold Briggs, who insisted that no one should be moved into a New Village until that Village could be properly protected. This meant a massive expansion of the police, who, fortunately for the Government, could be recruited from the Malay population who were hostile to a takeover by the Chinese communists. General Briggs insisted that a police post should be established in the Village before anyone was moved into it. This made it much more difficult for the M.C.P. cadres to operate in the New Villages, and brought home perhaps the most important lesson of the Malayan Emergency—that the villager is more subject to terror by the 'man with a knife' living inside the village at night than by the guerrilla with a gun coming in from the jungle outside.

The peak of the guerrilla phase occurred while this resettlement was being carried out, and in 1950 and 1951 about 100 civilians were being killed every month and a similar number of soldiers and policemen. Thereafter, far from being able to escalate into mobile war, the guerrilla campaign gradually lost ground until, by 1953, civilian casualties were down to 20 killed per month while the guerrillas themselves were losing over 100 per month.

As well as the eight guerrilla regiments, the M.C.P. also had to maintain their political structure in the jungle, because security in the villages was such that they ran too great a risk of arrest. Deep in the jungle was Chin Peng's Central Committee. Under this was a hierarchy of State and District Committees, leading down to the Branch Committees on the fringe of the jungle. These made contact across the jungle fringe with the cadres who lived in the Chinese villages and organized the food supply and other support for the guerrillas.

There was thus a complete 'parallel hierarchy' of revolutionary government, competing for control of the population with the Government of the country, which also had its hierarchy of State and District administrations leading down to the police post in the village itself. Another decisive lesson from the Government's victory was their realization that the destruction of this parallel hierarchy was more important than the destruction of the guerrilla regiments themselves, since without an effective organization which they respected and feared, the great majority of the population, even in the Chinese villages, would not wish to take the risk of supplying food or otherwise actively supporting the guerrillas.

Since the guerrillas could not live healthily on jungle produce alone, it was essential for them to smuggle food from the villages, along with other necessities such as ammunition (stolen or corruptly purchased from the police), clothing, paper for propaganda, radios, torch batteries, etc. By far the most important item was rice, for which there was no substitute, as the morale of the guerrillas rapidly fell if they were short of it.

A typical guerrilla Branch Committee on the jungle fringe would be five to ten strong, but would be responsible for smuggling food for about fifty in the higher committees and in the platoons of the regiment operating in their vicinity. This required at a minimum 250 lb. of rice per week. The Branch would collect this from four or five villages which would typically contain in all about 100 cadres, or 'Masses' Executives', whose job was to organize those members of the village population on whom they thought they could rely not to betray them. Again, a fairly typical number of villagers on whom any one Masses' Executive might rely would be ten, many of these being his own brothers or uncles or cousins, or relations of the men in the jungle. There was a very powerful family element at work and this was the best insurance against betrayal.

Like Mao Tse-Tung, Chin Peng wisely insisted that nothing should be taken from the people without payment, and this included the rice and the clothing, etc. That meant that the Branch Committee and the Masses' Executives also had a major task of collecting subscriptions. This was done partly by the extortion of protection money from small Chinese or Indian businessmen (owners of small holdings or operators of small bus companies). In exchange for immunity from ambush or destruction of his property, he would have to subscribe a substantial proportion of his profits—typically £100 to £300 per month. At the bottom end of the scale, the poorest rubber tapper might be required to hand over one per cent of his earnings—that is about 12p per month. As a striking example of this later in the Emergency, one Branch, which had been decimated down to only two devoted guerrillas, managed to collect £350 per week by a mixture of voluntary contributions and extortion.

With such money the M.C.P. were able not only to pay for their supplies, but also to provide pensions for the families of men killed in the jungle and other welfare payments. They were also able to run a number of front activities, both in the villages and amongst the older Chinese school children, amongst whom they recruited future cadres and guerrillas.

Of the run-of-the-mill suppliers amongst the rubber tappers, however, by no means all were family relations or loyal volunteers. Many of the others were initially coerced into smuggling food out of the village to little hidden dumps in the rubber estates. For an isolated rubber tapper amongst the trees, there was only one answer to a man with a red star in his cap and a gun in his hand who asked: 'Are you a friend of the people?' Having once broken the strict Emergency laws by smuggling food, the victim was 'hooked' because, if he stopped smuggling and thereby became of no further use to the M.C.P., there was the threat that they would tip off the police and he would be prosecuted.

It was on this supply organization that the police Special Branch concentrated in order to provide the decisive ingredient for defeating the guerrillas—intelligence. By strict control of food, and by searching everyone leaving the village to work in the rubber estates, they narrowed down the number of suppliers and forced the guerrillas more and more to rely on coercing people whose heart was not really in it. The police would identify these and then recruit them as agents, willing to give information to break up the organization and get themselves off the hook. Rather than try to penetrate the organization, Special Branch concentrated on 'turning' those who were already in it, so that they could locate the dumps on the jungle fringe and ambush the guerrillas when they came to collect their supplies. This involved the agent in a big risk, so he was paid a big reward. The Chinese are practical people and more and more of them became convinced that this was the quickest way to get the war off their backs.

By 1953, the Branch organization, with its cadres in the villages, was suffering heavy casualties and the M.C.P. had to milk the guerrilla regiments to provide men to keep it going. By the time Malaya became independent in 1957, only ten per cent of the

2*

guerrillas were left in the surviving platoons of the regiments; the remaining ninety per cent were concentrating desperately on keeping open the political and supply organization across the jungle fringe—the parallel hierarchy.

The Government encouraged the process from 1953 onwards by lifting all restrictions from the villages in the areas where they felt that the M.C.P. organization had been sufficiently weakened. These were called White Areas, and in them the food restrictions were lifted, the people could move freely and were no longer searched when they went out to work. Though there was always a risk that this would enable the M.C.P. organization to revive, in fact it never did, because the people were so relieved to be rid of the war that the police could be sure of someone giving them information if the guerrillas tried to come back.

The final crumble was a slow process, and around the villages of Perak and Johore, tempered by their of resistance against the Japanese, the communists hung on with a religious dedication matching that of the early Christian martyrs.

By 1960, the whole of Malaya was a White Area, and all that remained was Chin Peng with 400 survivors who had withdrawn across the jungle frontier into South Thailand. During the next seven years they trained several thousand Chinese as guerrillas and cadres to resume the war when they felt that internal difficulties in Malaya—or Malaysia as it had become—made the time right. Guerrilla attacks began again in 1967 and the familiar names of villages like Chemor and Sungei Siput began to reappear in the news.

The Government won the war in Malaya in the 1950s firstly because they provided adequate protection for the people in the form of a police post in every village; secondly because this gave that element of the population which did not want a communist victory, or which was apathetic and wished to be rid of the war, sufficient confidence to be prepared to give information. By concentrating on the supply organization, the Special Branch provided a means of harnessing this intelligence, and the army used it to eliminate the guerrillas at their point of contact with the people.

In 1959, when the Emergency in Malaya was coming to an end, the war in South Vietnam had begun again and was getting into its stride. At the Geneva Conference, which coincided with General Giap's victory at Dien Bien Phu, Vietnam had been partitioned, but Ho Chi Minh, to his great disappointment, acquired only the northern half. This was largely at the behest of Chou En-Lai, because the Chinese were already worried about the prospect of Russian influence in North Vietnam.

The French withdrew from South Vietnam and the Emperor Bao Dai was replaced by President Diem, who asked for American military and other advisers to help him to build up his army to defend his country against the expected onslaught from the North. Future historians may be surprised that it was over twenty years before the conquest was complete.

Initially the number of American military advisers was small—about seventy. And by 1959 there were still less than 400.

Meanwhile, Ho Chi Minh was preparing to carry out the conquest of the South by the same means that he had used in the North. At the time of partition, one million refugees, mainly Catholics, moved from the North into the South, and amongst these, Ho Chi Minh infiltrated cadres to begin the creation of a village organization which had thus far been confined largely to the North. At the same time his agents recruited small clandestine guerrilla groups from amongst the villagers.

This process was conducted by agit-prop teams, as earlier in China and North Vietnam. These have been brilliantly described by Malcolm Browne in his book *The New Face of War* (London, Cassell, 1966). A handful of young travellers would ask for hospitality in a village. They would help with the harvest or whatever else was happening and go on their way with invitations to call again next time they were passing. This they would do and would get into conversation with the villagers, telling them how much more the government should be doing for them, and how much better they could live if they saw the light. There were no police posts and the government presence in the villages had always been very thin, so Diem had little idea of what was going on.

The terror began in about 1957. Government officials who would not 'live and let live' were killed and so were informers. The next three years followed a pattern not unlike that of the start of the Malayan Emergency. In the three years 1948–50 in Malaya, the numbers of civilians killed were 500, 700 and 1,200. In South Vietnam, in the three years 1957–59, the numbers of civilians killed were 700, 1,200 and 2,500. Bearing in mind that South Vietnam had double the population of Malaya, the scale was roughly similar. Thereafter, however, things moved in opposite directions; in Malaya civilian killings in 1951 went down to 1,000 but in South Vietnam in 1960 they soared to 4,000 and went on rising.

One reason for this contrast was that the South Vietnamese Army, after 1954, had been trained primarily to defeat a North Vietnamese invasion like the invasion of South Korea by North Korea four years earlier, which was still fresh in people's minds. Fresh also was the memory of the 'mobile war' phase in North Vietnam in 1953–54. The American advisers, therefore, were training an army in 1955–59 which would have been suitable for Korea, and which ironically would have been suitable to meet the invading armies of North Vietnam in 1972 and 1975; it was, however, quite unsuitable, both in training and equipment, to deal with internal war. A far more important reason for the contrast in the course of events, however, was that at no time in South Vietnam was there a system of police posts in every village such as had been installed in Malaya. This meant that government officials and their collaborators were completely unprotected at night from the cadres and from the embryonic guerrilla units themselves, which were able to live quite freely in the villages.

As the years went by, these part-time guerrilla units, known as Popular Forces, grew, and provided recruits for full-time Regional Forces which began to form and train in jungle camps like those in Malaya. The Regional Forces in turn passed on their best men on completion of training to larger Regular Forces based deeper in the jungle. The Popular Forces were generally of squad or platoon size (ten to thirty), the Regional Forces of company size (about one hundred), while the Regular Forces were of battalion, regimental and later divisional size.

By 1961, both the South Vietnamese Government and the newly elected President Kennedy realized the seriousness of the situation and there was a rapid build-up of U.S. advisers. Kennedy instructed these advisers to switch the emphasis from defence against invasion to what became in U.S. parlance 'counterinsurgency'. The Special Warfare School was established at Fort Bragg, and a jungle warfare school in Panama.

A particular study was made of the communist defeat in Malaya, and a British Advisory Team under Mr. (later Sir) Robert Thompson was established in Saigon at the request of President Diem. A mammoth resettlement scheme was started under the dynamic guidance of President Diem's brother-in-law, but, in disregard of Thompson's advice, serious mistakes were made.

The first 'Strategic Hamlets' were set up not in the areas where the communists were weakest, as they had been in Malaya, but in the areas where they were strongest. As a result, they were quickly overrun and the scheme discredited from the start—in contrast to the steady spread of White Areas in Malaya from the most peaceful parts until all efforts could be concentrated on the toughest areas at the end.

The second mistake was the unrealistic pace at which the resettlement was attempted. No less than 12,000 Strategic Hamlets were established within two years, by contrast with 410 New Villages in Malaya in eighteen months. Most of these Strategic Hamlets did not even have a fence round them before the people were moved into them, and they themselves were instructed to erect a bamboo *panji* obstacle around the perimeter.

The worst mistake of all, however, was that no police posts, or army posts, were established in the Strategic Hamlets. Even the local part-time 'Home Guard' (also known rather confusingly as Popular Forces like those of the Viet Cong) were located outside the perimeters of the Strategic Hamlets. As with the French ten years earlier (in the north), the soldiers slept inside these detached fortresses, with their families, surrounded by barbed wire, and only ventured out by day. As a result, the only Popular Forces living inside the Strategic Hamlets were those of the Viet Cong. Anyone who toyed with the idea of giving active co-operation to the government soon had second thoughts.

At the end of 1963, when this ill-starred programme was nearing completion, both President Kennedy and President Diem were assassinated. During the next year there were no less than eight changes of government in Vietnam, and their support from the United States was guided by a man whom historians may see as their most disastrous President of all time—Lyndon B. Johnson.

In 1964, things had moved so fast that General Giap decided that the time had come to escalate to phase three, mobile war. The Regional and Regular Forces of the Viet Cong, however, had not by then reached a stage of development in which they could exploit the opportunity, so battalions of the North Vietnamese Regular Army moved down the Ho Chi Minh Trail through Eastern Laos and Cambodia into South Vietnam for the kill. By the end of 1964, despite a massive increase in the number of U.S. advisers, the end seemed to be in sight. Using the pretext of a naval incident in the Gulf of Tongking, President Johnson ordered the bombing of North Vietnam by U.S. aircraft, and shortly afterwards warned that if there were any more major raids on the bases where the U.S. advisers were living, Hanoi itself would be bombed. The raids continued and, with timing of incredible ineptitude, President Johnson ordered the bombing of Hanoi while Premier Kosygin was in the city, thereby ensuring that the Soviet Union publicly committed itself to supporting the North Vietnamese.

Shortly afterwards, U.S. combat troops landed, and within a year had built up to a strength of half a million men. The North Vietnamese Regular Army built up in parallel, until, by 1967, ninety per cent of the armed men fighting against the Americans and the South Vietnamese Army were North Vietnamese regular soldiers. The war had become a limited war, costing sometimes 500 American dead in a single week, and this the American public was not prepared to sustain. Peace negotiations began in 1968, and all U.S. combat units had withdrawn by 1971. The whole of Indo-China was in communist hands by 1975.

The guerrilla war moved into phase three in 1964 and was never thereafter more than a subsidiary to conventional operations at battalion and divisional strength. Although it took the North Vietnamese ten more years to win this conventional war, the very transition into phase three proved that they had won the guerrilla war by 1964.

There were, of course, fundamental differences between Vietnam and Malaya: in Vietnam, there was no equivalent of the forty-nine per cent Malay element of the population, who had no time for Chinese guerrillas, and supplied recruits for the Malayan Army and the police who could be relied upon not to defect or to betray the government; the terrain was different, and so was the relationship between the Malayan Government and the British; there was also a long tradition of administration down to village level in Malaya which there never had been in Vietnam.

Nevertheless, the South Vietnamese and American defeat in the guerrilla war was for precisely the inverse reasons for the government's success in Malaya. Firstly, the Vietnamese failed to provide security for the rural population, specifically as a result of their failure to establish police posts in the villages. As a direct consequence of this, they received little or no intelligence. For these two reasons the government structure at district and village level, so far as it existed at all, was unable to function, so the government's writ did not run. It was the parallel hierarchy of the Viet Cong which really governed the villages.

Underlying all these mistakes lay the failure of the Americans and the South Vietnamese to realize that it was this parallel hierarchy which mattered, not the combat units in the jungle. Mao Tse-Tung had been one of the first to realize that the function of a guerrilla army is to enable the Party to exercise political control over the people, and thereby to supplant the 'legitimate' government. It was because Chin Peng had been prevented from doing this that he failed, and it was because Ho and Giap were able to do it, both in the 1946–54 war and in the 1957–64 war, that they won.

4 Peaceful use of military forces

If guerrilla warfare and terrorism are the form of conflict for our time, then soldiers and policemen too are here to stay. Moreover, whether or not the world will continue to avoid nuclear war, it shows no sign of avoiding limited and civil wars. There has been no year since 1945 when there has not been at least one such war in progress and the 1973 Arab–Israeli War, the 1974 Cyprus War, the 1975 Indo-China War, and the 1976 civil wars in Lebanon and Angola suggest they are likely to continue.

Put another way, so long as there is crime, people will still need locks on their doors, even though there may be a thousand locks which are never forced for every one that is. So long as there are fires, fire precautions will still be needed, even though many a hose will never be used and fire brigades spend more time waiting than on active duty.

So it is with soldiers. It takes a long time to train a soldier and still longer to build up an efficient army, particularly one to deal with guerrilla warfare and terrorism. If the process is not begun until the attack is imminent it will be too late. Armies, therefore, like fire brigades, spend a minority of their time actually fighting. During their peaceful interludes, they have tremendous potential for constructive work, which is all too often wasted.

They are particularly valuable for working in the remotest areas, because army units are designed to live anywhere and to take care of themselves. They can, moreover, help to reduce the suffering and deprivation which provide the grounds for guerrilla warfare and terrorism. This may cause anger and frustration amongst revolutionaries, but not amongst the people who are hungry and deprived.

The principal underlying cause of violence in the world, and especially the guerrilla and terrorist violence, is the inequitable

48

distribution of wealth. The rich countries, like the U.S.A., Sweden, and the Arab oil states, have a *per capita* income of about thirty times that of the poorest countries in Africa and Asia. In most of the developed countries, the difference between the rewards of management and labour is nothing like so stark as this. Though nearly all have a small number of very rich people, their wealth, even if obscene and abrasive, would not go very far if split up amongst the rest of the population. Between average professional and managerial salaries and average manual workers' wages, taxation over the past century has brought the differentials down to 4, 5, or at most about 8 to 1. These ratios apply as much in Russia as in West European countries, but they do not apply in many of the developing countries, with the exception of China. In developing countries, the normal pattern is much more like that between the rich and the poor states—that is a ratio of something like 30 to 1 between the rewards of management and labour. This is because the development in these countries has been in the cities and very little has been done to develop the remote areas. As a result, much of the rural population is bitterly poor, and those members of it who are drawn towards the rapidly expanding cities in the hope of finding something better often end up in shanty towns, with no work, and in many ways more deprived than they were in their villages. It is no surprise that most rural guerrilla wars take place in countries like these. And it is precisely in the remote rural areas of such countries that soldiers are particularly well fitted to make a constructive contribution.

In these remote areas, the people have such a hard struggle to keep alive that there is little prospect of development. Sir Robert Thompson has suggested priorities for development work in such areas. First in importance is to train local people in technical and administrative skills. Second is to develop communications— roads, railways, air strips, and telecommunications. Third is to develop the rural economy, that is, agriculture and rural industries. And fourth is to improve social services, schools, clinics, etc. Many people would put social services first, but Sir Robert's argument is that it is useless to create social services which cannot continue to support themselves after the aid project which creates them has finished. This will only be possible on a permanent basis if the area can raise enough revenue to pay their running costs without being a drain on the rest of the community. Hence the higher priority for a thriving rural economy. This, however, can only be developed if communications are opened to enable improved agricultural equipment and fertilizers to be transported in and surplus produce to be transported to market— if it cannot, there is no point in growing surplus produce so the people will remain at subsistence level. Finally, none of these things will work unless local people are trained in the techniques and skills required to replace the foreign experts when they leave.

Soldiers can do many of these things. In some developing countries, such as Iran, a proportion of soldiers spend their con- scripted service in training and educating people in remote areas where it would be difficult to provide and maintain other teachers. Taking the second priority, armies are particularly well equipped to build basic roads out of local materials (rather than concrete highways) and bridges or, if necessary, ropeways, and air strips. Army signal units can provide telephone and radio communica- tions and can at the same time train local people to operate the equipment when they go. In other words, soldiers are well able to provide the infrastructure on which rural development can be based, in cases where it would be difficult to get civilian labour to work and to house or feed itself.

In remote areas, it is axiomatic that individual soldiers and individual villagers or tribesmen get on well together. The soldiers—many themselves having experienced hardship in their lives—sympathize with the people they are helping and find satisfaction in doing so. The people appreciate their work and delight in asking the soldiers into their homes and this in turn is appreciated by young men who are far away from their own homes and families.

This natural affinity was one of the main features of the Long March of Mao Tse-Tung's army to set up his base in Shensi in 1934–36; and it was the foundation of the strength of this army throughout the revolution.

After he had established control over the whole of China, Mao Tse-Tung did not disband the People's Liberation Army (P.L.A.). It is, to this day, some two and a half million strong, supplemented by a vast militia all over the country. It has sometimes been used for internal security (for example, during the Cultural Revolution), but it is primarily kept in being because of the intense fear the Chinese have of Russian invasion. There is no question of them taking the locks off their doors or disbanding their fire brigades. Meanwhile, however, the soldiers of the P.L.A. do a great deal to help the people, by carrying out major projects, such as railway and bridge construction in remote areas, and providing local assistance with the harvest or with flood prevention and disaster relief. Every army unit runs a farm in its base camp, in which all the soldiers on completion of training do a tour of duty. The P.L.A. medical units provide clinics and also run six-week courses for people in remote villages to act as 'barefoot doctors', able to carry out treatment of simple ailments and provide first aid.

The peaceful use of military forces, however, goes back a good deal further than that. The Romans certainly used their army in this way, and they found that when the soldiers were doing constructive work which was clearly of benefit to the people, this did a great deal to make their presence acceptable and to keep the peace. If a minority turned to violence so that the soldiers had to stop constructive work to fight, the majority resented this and were on the side of the soldiers.

The United States Army played a big part in opening up the West, and much constructive work was done, not only by the Corps of Engineers, but also by the Infantry and Cavalry. In 1820 Zachary Taylor wrote in a letter to the Quartermaster General: 'The axe, pick, saw and trowel have become more the implement of the American soldier than the cannon, musket and sword.' The British Army also did a great deal of constructive work during the years of Empire and this helped to get the soldier his reputation as 'Britain's best ambassador'.

Many undeveloped countries in Africa, Asia and Latin America also use their armies for rural development, though they are frequently diverted by external confrontations and internal disturbance. Whatever the justification for these latter, they do have the effect of delaying much needed development.

There is, in addition, great scope for soldiers from the industrialized world to do constructive work in the remote areas of underdeveloped countries, and this is more welcome than most people would imagine, provided that the soldiers are unarmed and are clearly not acting in a combatant role. The British Army does a great deal of this, and in 1968–70, such projects were conducted in thirty-four different developing countries, including Bangladesh, Ethiopia, Guyana, Kenya, Malawi, Peru and Zaire. The British Army also helped in disaster relief all over the world, and its work after the earthquake in Skopje in Yugoslavia will be particularly remembered. Three projects may be worth describing, the first in Malaya in the 1950s, and the other two in Thailand in the 1960s.

In an earlier chapter the withdrawal of Chin Peng, with the headquarters of the Malayan Communist Party, from Malaya into South Thailand in the latter years of the Emergency was described. The border country on the Malayan side consisted of mountainous jungle in which there were a number of steep valleys where small communities lived, growing rice and catching fish and wild animals for their own needs. These were mainly of mixed Thai and Malay blood and they were known as Sum-Sums. To many Western people, exhausted by the roar of life in a modern city, the existence of the Sum-Sums might sound idyllic. Most of them, however, did not find it so. Subsistence agriculture can be a hard and boring life. They had no access to market for any surplus crops, no access to doctors if they were ill or injured, and no access to schools for their children. Above all, they had no options whatever in how they spent their days unless they abandoned their roots and their extended families and started a new life in what would be for them an alien community. The government could do little for them, because they were entirely cut off except for jungle trails.

For the Malayan Communist Party in the border area, however, they were a boon. The guerrillas lived in jungle camps, and relied upon the Sum-Sum settlements for food, in exchange for which they, following the example of the P.L.A. in China, sent their 'barefoot doctors' to help the people when they were in trouble. It was a straightforward competition in government, in which only the M.C.P. held any cards. For all that, the services the guerrillas could provide filled only a minute proportion of the Sum-Sums' needs. Only the government could really improve their lot, and then only if it could get access to them.

The answer lay in construction of roads. The existing road system petered out in a series of fingers going up the valleys into the jungle. The answer was to extend these in a series of arcs twisting their way through as many Sum-Sum settlements as possible and linking up the ends of these fingers. This amounted to sixty-four miles of basic country roads made of laterite, a kind of self-binding soil available in seams all along the route. There were many streams to cross, requiring bridges and culverts, and a number of formidable rivers which needed strong reinforced concrete bridges able to stand up to a raging torrent in the flash floods of the monsoon.

For a number of reasons, only soldiers could tackle this task. Being close to the guerrillas' main base camps, including those beyond the frontier, the construction teams would be liable to heavy attack. Civilian contractors would have found it almost impossible either to recruit or to maintain a labour force in such country. The task was begun by a squadron of British troops, and continued over the next two years by Gurkha and Malayan soldiers.

The project fulfilled its expectations. The Sum-Sums extended their cultivations because, with transport calling regularly for produce, there was now some point in growing more than was needed for their own consumption. Mobile clinics paid regular visits, primary schools were established and, as the years went by, older children were able to get by bus to secondary schools in the towns. These were the things which the people wanted and they resented anyone impeding their completion, so when guerrillas tried to continue their contacts the people informed the police.

There was therefore a security by-product. The guerrillas, now able to obtain food only from Thailand, were forced to abandon such camps as they had in range of the farming and rubber growing areas of north Malaya where there were Chinese communities whose control was the M.C.P.'s real target. Mao Tse-Tung's strategy was therefore operating in reverse. Instead of working inwards from the remote areas towards the more prosperous agricultural and cash crop communities until the cities were encircled by the hostile countryside, the guerrillas were being driven back by denial of sources of food into the deep jungle where they could exercise no political control, and finally across the border into Thailand, where they were to remain for the next ten years.

During these ten years, the Malayan Government further extended the road system, adding an all-weather tarmac surface, and when Chin Peng did resume his incursion into Malaysia in 1967, he did so by setting up jungle camps down the mountainous central spine of Malaya closer to his traditional hard-core Chinese supporters in Perak, but without the advantage which Giap had been able to enjoy in Indo-China in 1950–54 of operating from a sanctuary beyond the frontier. The war continued, but the Sum-Sums were largely free of it.

In the late 1960s a project of a very different kind was going on in another part of Thailand, close to the Burmese border, not far from the famous bridge over the River Kwai. Here the problem was water, and the task allotted to a very small team of about a dozen British soldiers fell primarily into the first priority of the four quoted earlier—that is, to train local people in the technical skills required for drilling deep wells. British soldiers took their own drilling rigs with them and left them behind after drilling the first few wells, having by then trained local teams to operate them. With the team were a number of building tradesmen, who built a new school from local materials, again involving the inhabitants of the largest village in the district, who were thereafter able to enhance their traditional building methods with some additional techniques.

Most of the twelve soldiers were Royal Engineers, but it is worth mentioning one who was not. He was a trooper of the Special Air Service (S.A.S.) whose deployment (whether in Oman or in Northern Ireland) has so often reduced writers with revolutionary sympathies to near apoplexy. There was nothing clandestine about the work of this soldier, who wore S.A.S. uniform and badges. Like many S.A.S. troopers, he had voluntarily relinquished N.C.O. rank (in his case as a Sergeant in the Coldstream Guards) for an exciting life in far-away places. The particular skills he brought to western Thailand were an interpretership in the Thai language and training as a medical orderly—in other words, as a 'barefoot doctor'. His eleven healthy British comrades required little medical attention; the Thais needed it desperately. They came in from the villages far and wide as his reputation spread and he treated on average a hundred Thais a week. He continually demanded extra medical equipment, sometimes with alarming implications—such as a pair of dentist's pincers. These were provided, despite his lack of formal qualifications as a dental surgeon, because he was in any case tugging out rotten teeth with a pair of pliers rather than allowing them to produce a possibly fatal abscess. He was warned to be careful not to kill anyone, lest his magic be misinterpreted as malignant, but he never did. He safely delivered babies, treated every kind of injury and disease, and saved many lives. He was the best loved man in the village and, though there were guerrillas about, he never had to carry a gun. If they had laid a hand on him—or, for that matter, on any of the well drillers—they would have got short shrift from the villagers.

It is worth mentioning that the S.A.S. in a much more violent situation in Oman in 1970–75, as well as helping to train the local forces and going out with them on anti-guerrilla operations, frequently lived in groups of four or five in Arab villages, helping them in similar ways, both medically and technically, and were again sometimes accompanied by sapper well-drilling teams. They occasionally suffered casualties in battles with the guerrillas in the mountains, but none was ever attacked in the villages. The inhabitants saw to it that they were 'fish in a friendly sea'.

A larger British Army project in Thailand—this time in the north-east, took place in 1966–68. This was close to the Mekong River, which forms the border with Laos, and the population includes a small North Vietnamese minority. For over a thousand years the North Vietnamese (or Tongkinese) have coveted both Laos and the plateau west of the Mekong, over which the Tongkinese and the Thais have historically fought. There was at this time an active guerrilla movement in the area, the guerrillas and cadres being trained in a special camp at Hoa Binh, near Hanoi, which trained 130 Thai-speaking students at a time.

The British Army project took place in the district of Loeng Nok Tha, which had a population of 50,000. Through the district ran a single road built of laterite which remained just passable during both wet and dry seasons. Only twenty-five per cent of the population lived within reasonable range of this road. The other seventy-five per cent had no access to anything other than paths, which were flooded for large parts of the year. Their condition, therefore, was not unlike that of the Sum-Sums in Malaya; they had no access to market, to doctors or to secondary schools (in this case there were primary school teachers in most of the villages) or to anything better than subsistence agriculture unless they abandoned their family roots and joined the growing throng of disillusioned peasants on the outskirts of the big cities—a pattern sadly familiar in Africa and Latin America as well as Asia.

In 1966, about one hundred guerrillas, graduates from the Hoa Binh school, were operating in the district, in two bands of fifty each. During the first four months of the year, police casualties were heavy, seven out of thirty-eight being killed. Most of these were ambushed in attempting to carry the government's writ to outlying villages. Apart from the casualties (nearly one in five during four months) they were hampered by the lack of roads. As a result, by April 1966, the guerrillas had virtual control of the entire countryside except for the immediate vicinity of the village of Loeng Nok Tha itself. There was no doubt about who was winning the 'competition in government' here. Yet it was not what the people wanted. Under their traditional system of land tenure, each family owned the paddy-fields it cultivated, and they did not want to be collectivized, as the communist guerrillas promised they would be 'after the revolution'. Nor did they want to be ruled by a movement which, although manned by Thais, had its headquarters in Hanoi. They had been resisting this for ten centuries.

The recruitment of the Thai guerrillas and cadres followed the familiar agit-prop pattern, and was well described by a defector, Panna Porn, who told his story to the *Bangkok Post* in 1966. Panna was a young man, frustrated at the prospect of a life of subsistence agriculture, with six months of backbreaking toil in the wet season, and six months of boredom in an isolated village in the dry season. The agit-prop man was a North Vietnamese travelling apothecary who asked him whether he had no ambition to do anything other than this. Panna replied that he had always wanted to be a doctor. The North Vietnamese said that there would be little hope of this without education, which of course he could never get in Thailand, but which he could get if he were willing to go to 'a more enlightened country' for a few months. Panna was interested, so he was advised to tell his parents that he was heading north in search of a job, but in fact to go to a rendezvous on the banks of the Mekong to be ferried across for the eighteen-day walk through the mountains of Laos to Hoa Binh.

When he got there, Panna found that the eight-month course comprised six months' political indoctrination and two months' weapon training and guerrilla tactics. None of it seemed to have much to do with becoming a doctor. At the end of it he was told to return to his village and await instructions to set up a clandestine organization to support the guerrillas. But Panna was disillusioned and his parents did not believe his story about going to look for a job. So he was one of the cadres who defected and told his story to the police.

Nevertheless, there were others who did not, and there seemed every likelihood in 1966 of the guerrillas extending their control, soon into Loeng Nok Tha village, and then linking up with neighbouring districts until the police and government officials were driven out altogether and the cities were surrounded by a hostile countryside.

As with the Sum-Sums in Malaya, the first stage of the cure was to build roads, and for similar reasons this was done by soldiers. Pushing out from Loeng Nok Tha, a Thai Army team headed in one direction, and the British Army team in another. Within one and a half years, the twenty-five per cent with access to roads had risen to seventy-five per cent.

The British Army team consisted of about 200 soldiers. As they went, they were joined by 200 Thai villagers, whose wages were paid by the Thai Government, and who learned road-making skills on the job. They built thirty miles of road in fifteen months, including fourteen bridges and ninety-three culverts. Concrete mixers and moulds for building culvert pipes were set up in the army camp and manned entirely by Thais, who kept the equipment, and the skills, when the soldiers had gone. Other Thais learned the skills of using explosives to blast the roots and fell the giant trees in the jungle sections of the route. Perhaps most impressive of all were two villagers who, in the course of a year, learned to use surveying instruments to set out the road, the last part of which they did independently with no British supervision at all. The necessary plant to maintain the road was also left behind, and seven years later, in 1975, the British military attaché drove along the road, finding it still in good order.

This piece of foreign aid cost the British Foreign Office (who financed the project) £218,000. Compared with simultaneous road projects by civil contractors in less remote areas of Thailand, the road was built at twice the speed and half the cost per mile of any other. One good reason for this was that the whole project made sense to the soldiers themselves. Although the temperature was over 100°F, soldiers who had been on shift from 5 a.m. till noon would volunteer to do the afternoon shift as well (and soldiers do not get paid overtime). They were inspired by the reception they received in the villages as they worked. Everywhere they were asked into people's homes. When a small group of them learned of the disappointment of a village which the road missed by two miles, they asked if they could use the plant in their spare time to build a spur road to it, and then subscribed spontaneously to run a children's party in the village to celebrate its completion.

The soldiers wore uniforms but carried no guns, despite the security situation in the district. Once again, it was clear that the villagers would have had no truck with any guerrilla who attacked one of these soldiers, and none of them ever did.

This illustrates a principle put into words by Evan Luard, Labour M.P. and one-time Junior Minister in the Foreign Office, that the most effective form of aid is that which would be of equal value whether there were a revolution or not. This certainly applied to the road, and it amused the soldiers to hear of an inter-cepted broadcast from the 'Free Thai' radio operating from Laos, instructing the guerrillas not to attack the British soldiers because the road would be useful to the people after the revolution.

The road advanced, but the revolution did not. By the time it was finished the one hundred guerrillas had been reduced to nineteen. This was not because of military action—no Thai soldiers moved along the road until they came to guard the Minister who conducted its formal opening. The change came because the people rejected the guerrillas and quickly reported their move-ments to the police, who in turn suffered no more casualties and were able to move freely throughout the district.

Like the well drillers on the Burmese border, the British soldiers brought by-products to North-East Thailand. They had a doctor with them—not a barefoot doctor this time—and he treated 1,500 Thais a week, running a mobile clinic. They also dug wells, initially installing only hand-pumps, because it was no use putting in motor-pumps until the villagers had acquired the skills to operate and maintain them. These followed a year later, when buses and trucks were regularly using the road, and mechanics had begun to appear in the villages.

Six months before the road was completed twenty-six buses per day were running from Loeng Nok Tha to the villages it had reached so far. A clinic was regularly visiting each village, and one community had already imported materials to make a concrete catchment system and storage tank to build up rain-water for the dry season. Older children were taking the bus to secondary schools and young people seeking technical education and better jobs. A covered market was being constructed at the crossroads from which the road set off, to receive the surplus produce which the people had already started to grow.

As in Malaya, there are still guerrillas in North East Thailand and, though they may still get support from North Vietnam, they get none from China, which has established friendly relations with the Government of Thailand. There is a better hope of peace and prosperity for the people of Loeng Nok Tha than there was ten years ago when the British soldiers started to build their road, and the soldiers themselves will remember that, for this part of their army service at least, they were doing something constructive.

The multiple purpose of projects such as those described is evident. Life in the remote areas of the world is not a bed of roses, whatever some people living in comfort may believe. People living at subsistence level try to break out, either by disastrous migration to the outskirts of overcrowded cities, or by supporting violent men who promise them a new way of life. Whatever may be their political future, the people benefit from roads, bridges and water supply. They also benefit from the skills they acquire from the soldiers. Where the soldiers are indigenous (like the Thai Army detachment building the other road in Loeng Nok Tha) they improve their relations with their own people. Where they are foreign soldiers they improve relations between their countries. They also gain in every way from using other means than fighting, when the situation permits, to achieve the soldiers' most rewarding aim—to stop people killing each other.

5 Northern Ireland

So much has been written about Northern Ireland, like South East Asia, that the essentials have become obscured. This has been made worse by the fact that almost all those who write are, with varying degrees of passion, partisans of one side or the other.

Northern Ireland, however, is of unique interest to the student of political violence for a number of reasons. Firstly, though most of the killing has been in the urban environment of Belfast, a significant proportion of it has been in remote rural areas near the border with the Republic, especially in South Armagh. Secondly, the terrorists of both sides are recruited almost wholly from the deprived sectors of the two communities. While all revolutionary movements claim to be or to represent the 'working class', the Provisional I.R.A. and the Ulster Volunteer Force (U.V.F.) seem to be the only ones in the world which are recruited from it.

Thirdly, neither of the main Protestant and Catholic terrorist movements have any detectable political ideology and seem to be motivated solely by nationalist or sectarian aims. Though the Official I.R.A. have a Marxist philosophy, they have used relatively little violence since 1972. The Provisional I.R.A. (who are, incidentally, much closer to the 'traditional' I.R.A. than the Officials) aim primarily to sicken the British Government and the British public of the task of administering the Province so that they will go away. Their secondary aim is the sectarian one of terrorizing the Protestant population in the hope of weakening support for the U.V.F.—and this may well have overtaken the primary nationalist aim in 1975; and the third aim is a factional one of similarly weakening and terrorizing the supporters of their Catholic rivals, the Official I.R.A. The aim of the U.V.F. is almost wholly the sectarian one of thinning the ranks of the Provisionals and terrorizing the supporters of both wings of the I.R.A.; there is some factional strife in the Protestant movements, and they too might at any time themselves take on the nationalist aim of sickening the British and driving them away, if they were ever to feel that they would get on better as an independent State.

Finally, because the violence on both sides has stemmed from communal strife rather than political ideology, it is far more deeply rooted in history than is the case with revolutionary movements elsewhere in the world, whose philosophy can be traced back only to nineteenth-century Marxism or anarchism or, at the very earliest, to the eighteenth century. By contrast, the roots of communal strife in Ireland go back certainly to the year 1600 and, it could be argued, to the first English interference in the island in the twelfth century.

In creating intractable communal problems all over the world, the British seem to have no rivals in history. They attempted to form a unified sub-continent in India, instead of allowing it to take its natural course in shaking out into a Balkanized patchwork of independent states, with the result that over two million Hindus and Muslims killed each other in the process of independence, inflicting wounds which have never ceased to be septic. It was under British rule that Chinese and Indian labour migrated into Malaya, with the result that, when they inherited independence, the Malays made up only forty-nine per cent of the population of their country. It was largely under British administration that Greeks poured into Cyprus and outnumbered the indigenous Turks. The massive Jewish immigration into Palestine, which passed the point of no return in the 1930s, took place under the British mandate. And, of course, it was the migration of English and Scottish Protestants into a Catholic Ireland which created a problem which no government has been able to solve since Queen Elizabeth I sent in the English Army in 1601.

History is the biggest bugbear in Northern Ireland. Every child is brought up to remember it. 'Remember 1690' is painted on the walls all over the Province, but sadly no one thinks of appending '. . . but you are living in the 1970s'. The most fruitless of all occupations is trying to *re-write* history. Perhaps Queen Elizabeth I, or James I, or Cromwell, or William III, or Gladstone, or Carson, or Michael Collins, or Lloyd George ought not to have done this or that—but the fact is that they did and it cannot be undone. To comprehend Northern Ireland at all, however, it is vitally important to *understand* history.

Where should we start? In 1155 when the Pope (the only English Pope in history) placed Ireland under the rule of the English King? Or 1494, when the Irish Parliament, with much skulduggery, subordinated itself to the English Parliament? Or the occupation of the island by Queen Elizabeth's army in 1601?

Perhaps the best starting point is a few years after that—about 1605-10, when James I had ascended the throne, and was establishing Protestant settlers in Virginia and in Canada —and, of course, in Ireland. In the hope of ensuring a Protestant Ascendancy, he concentrated a large colony of Scottish settlers in Ulster. This was at a time when religious feeling between rival faiths was more passionate even than between rival Marxist faiths today. It was all the more passionate in Ireland because it coincided with national and racial feeling. James I was trying not only to impose an alien religion on the Irish, but also to take their land from them. They would have none of this. The Catholic religion became the focus of their resistance, and has remained so ever since. Cromwell was to feel the intensity of it during his ruthless suppression of the Irish in 1649-50.

The deepest scars of all, however, were inflicted in 1688-91, because they were injected with the poison of humiliation. James II, as bigoted a Catholic as his grandfather had been a Protestant, was ousted by the Protestant William of Orange. James escaped to Ireland and raised a Catholic army. William landed with a Protestant army and the Civil War lasted for over two years, though some would say it has still not ended after 300 years. Protestant victories like the defence and relief of Londonderry in 1689 and the Battle of the Boyne in 1690 are still celebrated every year in Northern Ireland, with the specific purpose of taunting and crowing over the Catholics.

Surprisingly, one of the attempted risings against the British which came nearest to success was led by a middle-class Protestant, Wolfe Tone, in 1798, with the support of revolutionary France. At about the same time, the Ulster Protestants formed the Orange Order to defend their religion. William Pitt tried to defuse the situation by emancipating the Catholics from discriminatory laws, but resigned when George III was persuaded to invoke his coronation oath to frustrate him. Catholic emancipation had to wait another thirty years.

In the 1840s, famine struck the island, and shipload after ship-load of embittered Irishmen migrated to the United States, carrying with them a hatred of everything English, which has been bequeathed to their descendants who form the majority of the twenty-two million Irish American community. There are, today, five Irishmen in America for every Irishman in Ireland, North and South combined, and it is they who provide the bulk of the money and the weapons to the Provisional I.R.A., despite passionate pleading not to do so by Ministers of every Party in every Dublin Government.

In 1886 Gladstone introduced a Home Rule Bill but failed to carry it through Parliament. He carried his second Home Rule Bill through the House of Commons in 1893 but it was defeated in the House of Lords. Since that date, many British Parliaments would have liked to find a way of ridding themselves of Ireland, but they were always frustrated by militant Ulster Protestants with the threat of civil war. It was one of these, Lord Carson, who in 1912 formed the Ulster Volunteer Force, whose name the modern U.V.F. assumed in 1966. Carson smuggled 40,000 rifles into the Province, and it is estimated that some 10,000 of these have been lovingly preserved to this day, wrapped in oily rags under the floorboards, ready for the civil war.

The Easter Rising of 1916 was the Catholics' 'Battle of the Boyne' and taught some lessons which should be taken to heart. A handful of fanatical Republicans seized the Post Office in Dublin, and proclaimed a Provisional Government, without any serious attempt to rally mass support beforehand. They were quickly overpowered and, since almost every family in Ireland had at least one relation fighting against the Germans in the trenches, the Rising was regarded as a stab in the back. The men who were later to become the greatest of all Irish martyrs went into captivity, and to their death, with nothing but the jeers of their compatriots ringing in their ears. The British Government, greatly enraged and unwilling to divert extra troops from the war-fronts, made the cardinal error of over-reacting from a position of weakness. The jeers turned to sympathy, and the sympathy to passion, which continued to grow until Michael Collins was able to harness it for the war of independence in 1919–21.

Michael Collins should have his place in history as a guerrilla leader, not only because he won, but also because he was one of the first to give highest priority to attacking the Government's intelligence organization. He killed ruthlessly and brutally, with the primary purpose of eliminating informers and deterring potential informers, and also of systematically eliminating Government intelligence officers. The British were eager to extricate themselves from Ireland anyway, so Michael Collins' guerrilla activities did little more than precipitate their decision, but the credit which this brought him established his leadership.

The Northern Protestants, however, were determined not to come under Irish rule and persuaded the British Government that the six Northern counties, which contained a Protestant majority, should remain in the United Kingdom. Collins, elected as Prime Minister in Ireland's first Dail, agreed to this, probably feeling that he would have enough on his hands in setting up the new Free State without saddling himself with a violently hostile community within it. In 1922, the twenty-six counties became independent, but Collins was blamed for failing to gain the other six counties by the Irish Republican Army which he himself had created and led, and they plunged the country into a civil war bloodier than any which occurred in Ireland, North or South, until the present conflict in the 1970s. Before 1922 was out, the I.R.A. had assassinated Collins himself, and since that day they have never ceased to be at war with the Government of their own country in Dublin. Even when what had been their own political party, Fianna Fail, came to power under De Valera, one of the few survivors of the Easter Rising, they continued to fight the Government, killing more Irishmen in the South than they did in the North.

Their activities were sporadic, and occasionally spread across into England, as in 1939, but their biggest campaign since the 1920s was the Border Campaign in 1956–62. This failed to attract Catholic support on either side of the border and was a fiasco. Inevitably the leadership was discredited and it was replaced by a new Marxist leadership, containing a proportion of intellectuals, committed with even greater determination to bringing down the

Government in Dublin; in fact to bringing down the whole structure of parliamentary democracy and substituting a Marxist republic. To this end, they regarded the reabsorption of the six counties of the North as incidental, necessary only to bring in an industrial counterweight to destabilize the predominantly agricultural, clerically dominated and traditional society in the South, which they realized was far from a revolutionary situation. For this purpose, their aim was not to fight the Protestants in the North, but to unite the Protestant and Catholic working classes in the Province, urging them to overthrow their Protestant middle-class leadership on class grounds. Their target was what they called the 'green Tories'—that is, all the political parties—in Dublin.

Meanwhile, politics in the North had settled, during the forty years 1922 to 1962, into a rigid polarization, the cardinal issue in every election being whether to remain in the United Kingdom or reunify with the South. Through the Orange Order, and by discrimination in favour of Protestants over employment, housing, etc., the Protestant leadership managed to retain the loyalty of the Protestant working class, who were convinced that they would lose these advantages if absorbed into the Republic. Since there were twice as many Protestant voters as Catholics, the result of every election was a foregone conclusion, and, under the British system of 'winner take all' the Catholic parties had no part in government.

This completely confounded the naïve hopes of the Westminster architects of partition in 1922. They had given considerable autonomy to the Stormont Government in Belfast in the hope that reunification would have a better chance of being worked out peacefully between Belfast and Dublin than between London and Dublin—between Irishmen and Irishmen, rather than between Englishmen and Irishmen.

In 1965, however, the first attempt to bridge the gap was made by Prime Ministers O'Neill in Stormont and Lemass in Dublin, who visited each other's capitals and extended commercial and other co-operation. Alarmed, the Reverend Ian Paisley denounced O'Neill for entertaining a 'Fenian Papist murderer' in the Province. Encouraged by O'Neill's attempts to eradicate discrimination, Catholics of all political colours, supported in the background

3

by the (now Marxist) I.R.A., formed a Northern Ireland Civil Rights Association (N.I.C.R.A.), which organized marches and demonstrations to demand quicker reforms than O'Neill was able to carry through. These marches were blocked by militant Protestants under Paisley, and the Royal Ulster Constabulary (R.U.C.) made the fatal error of failing to protect the right to demonstrate.

Early in 1969, eighty-seven marchers were admitted to hospital after a demonstration had been ambushed by Protestants with sticks and stones at Burntollet, near Londonderry. Although no one was killed, feelings were rising and continued to do so throughout the year. The Protestant celebration of the Battle of the Boyne ('Remember 1690') in July was followed by rising communal violence which was already extending the R.U.C. in Belfast when the 'Apprentice Boys' March' on 12th August caused violent rioting at the interface between the Protestant and Catholic sectors of Londonderry. At this point the Stormont Government reluctantly asked that British troops should be called in— reluctantly because they feared that this might eventually lead to direct rule from Westminster, which in fact it did two and a half years later.

The Catholics initially welcomed the soldiers on the streets, partly because they sensed that this represented an admission of defeat by the Stormont Government and the R.U.C., but more so because they felt that in the communal rioting the R.U.C. was on the side of the Protestants. During the rioting immediately before the army came in, ten people had been killed of whom eight were Catholics. The R.U.C. had armoured cars, and the Catholics accused them of deliberately breaking through the barricades at the entrances to Catholic areas to let in the Protestant mobs to kill and to burn. The R.U.C. were armed, but the Catholics were not, and the I.R.A., traditionally their protectors in rioting in Belfast, were not to be seen.

This was because the Marxist I.R.A. leaders were determined not to participate in any fighting between Protestant and Catholic working classes whom they hoped to unite. Laudable though this was, it was deeply resented by the traditional I.R.A. men and their supporters in the slum areas where the worst of the fighting had taken place—particularly in the Ardoyne district of Belfast.

Graffiti appeared on the walls 'I.R.A.—I Ran Away'. Angry traditionalists met together and, after a number of bitter meetings, broke away to form a new 'Provisional' I.R.A. (named to commemorate the Provisional Government proclaimed in the Dublin Post Office in 1916) wedded to the traditional I.R.A. aims: to beat the Protestants to their knees, drive out the British and reunify Ireland.

The Provisional I.R.A. realized that in communal rioting the Protestants would always have the advantage, so they decided to launch an urban guerrilla campaign. They had, however, to build up their organization and their arms and ammunition almost from nothing, so, apart from one unplanned clash in June, they generally lay low in 1970, organizing, equipping, and building up their support in the Catholic slum areas where it had always been strongest. The U.V.F., which had re-emerged in 1966 with some bombing and assassination operations as a reaction to O'Neill's overtures to Dublin, set about doing the same.

Both these two urban guerrilla movements built their support on communities which have a characteristic probably unique in the world: *both* the communities, Protestant and Catholic, feel and behave like embattled minorities.

In the six counties of Northern Ireland there are one million Protestants and half a million Catholics. Thus the Catholics are in a minority of thirty-three per cent. Having suffered from discrimination for fifty years, and been denied any part in the government of their country, they certainly are a minority with reason to feel embittered.

In the twenty-six counties of the South, there are another 200,000 Protestants, and 2·8 million Catholics. Thus, if Ireland were reunited, the thirty-two counties would contain 1·2 million Protestants and 3·3 million Catholics. The Protestants would then be in a minority of twenty-seven per cent. They have been in such a minority for 300 years. Before 1922, when all Ireland was part of the United Kingdom, they felt that their religion and their way of life—the Protestant Ascendency—would be protected. In a united Ireland, they know that they would not, which is why they always opposed Home Rule and reunification. Suspecting that both Dublin and London, not to mention their Catholic neighbours in the North, are working for a united Ireland, the

Ulster Protestants, like the Ulster Catholics, have all the complexes of a minority.

Religion is little more than a label. The real division is between settlers and natives. Ireland was colonized by English and Scots. In most colonies, the natives are brown and the settlers are white. In Ireland they are all the same colour, but the natives have clung fast to the vital difference of their religion, which the settlers came specifically to challenge.

Thus, Catholic and Protestant families send their children to different schools—the Catholics to their Church schools and the Protestants to the State schools. On the streets, the children have for centuries formed into rival gangs—again Catholic and Protestant. From these they graduate to teenage gangs armed first with knives and later with guns—children of thirteen are frequently found to be armed, and at least one ten-year-old has been picked up with a loaded pistol in his pocket.

Segregation is worst in the poorest areas. No matter how hard some local authorities have tried to mix the communities, as soon as fighting starts they quickly shake out into green and orange areas. Once it begins it gathers pace. The smaller the number of Catholics left in a Protestant area, the more vulnerable they feel and the harder they seek to move out. The comfortable suburbs stay mixed, but the slums, like the Ardoyne, the Shankill and the Lower Falls, have always bred rival gangs to fight each other, and their inhabitants are motivated by a territorial imperative which pervades the atmosphere.

Such areas provide a natural breeding ground, as well as secure bases, for the I.R.A. and the U.V.F. They also provide a field of battle for the sectarian murders which in 1975 supplanted bombing and gun battles as the main cause of violent death.

By January 1971 the Provisional I.R.A. was ready to begin its urban guerrilla campaign. Aiming to inflame its own supporters by arousing over-reaction and repression, they launched a bombing campaign which quickly escalated from thirty-seven major bomb explosions in April to ninety-one in July. A campaign of selective terror was mounted, to deter witnesses from giving evidence and juries from convicting. As a result, there were very few convictions. The bombers went free and the Protestant majority furiously demanded action.

It was in this climate of opinion that the Prime Minister, Mr. Brian Faulkner, urged the British Government to agree to the ill-advised decision to introduce internment without trial on 9th August 1971. He argued that, if this were not done, there was a serious risk of the Protestant population taking the law into their own hands.

The effect was disastrous. Of the 342 arrested on the first night, a substantial proportion had no proven connection with the I.R.A. and were quickly released. Of the remainder, twelve were interrogated 'in depth' which involved long periods of questioning, with frequent interruption of sleep and a bread and water diet; they were kept standing against the walls in 'search posture', sometimes with pillow-cases over their heads and background noise to stop them seeing or hearing the others who were being questioned. Though the amount of information obtained was considerable, this kind of ill-treatment aroused anger and criticism both inside and outside Northern Ireland. Interrogation is a slow business and requires much patience, especially if, as in this case, some of those arrested resist violently. For comparison, in major operations in Malaya, it was customary to limit the number of suspects arrested for interrogation in depth to twenty or twenty-five per month. Arresting 342 in one night vastly exceeded the capacity for interrogation in Northern Ireland.

The result was a rapid escalation of violence. Bombings in August rose to over 100 and reached a peak of 146 in January 1972. Moreover, while only fifty-nine people in all had been killed in the two years from August 1969 to 9th August 1971, a further 231 were killed in the following six months.

The results were predictable. British soldiers had carried out the arrests (though not the interrogation) and had borne the brunt of attempting to control the violence afterwards. The British Government told Mr. Faulkner that they were no longer willing for British troops to be used under the direction of the Stormont Government, and that responsibility for security would have to be shifted direct to London. Mr. Faulkner was unwilling to accept this and resigned. In March 1972 the Stormont Parliament was prorogued, and direct rule from Westminster was instituted under a Secretary of State for Northern Ireland in the British Cabinet, Mr. William Whitelaw. After almost exactly fifty years, Protestant

Unionist rule of Northern Ireland was at an end—a major triumph for the Provisional I.R.A.

If 1972 proved the military potential of the Provisional I.R.A., however, it also proved their political ineptitude. With such a triumph, they had the opportunity of ending their violence and leaving their political wing, the Sinn Fein, to negotiate a political settlement at the height of their prestige. Indeed, shortly after taking over, Mr. Whitelaw invited their leaders to London for discussions to this end. In the event, however, 1972 was the bloodiest year of the war, 467 being killed of whom 321 were civilians. Thirteen of these were killed by the British Army on 'Bloody Sunday' in January, when parachutists were unwisely launched to make arrests in a riot at a sensitive spot in Londonderry and became involved in a gun battle with the I.R.A. The great majority of the 321 civilians, however, were killed by I.R.A. bombings, of which some could only be described as lunacy from the point of view of influencing local and world public opinion against themselves. On 3rd January 1972, for example, a lorry-load of glass bottles was parked in one of the busiest shopping streets in Belfast with a time-bomb inside. Of the sixty-two wounded, fifty-five were predictably women and children. In March a suit-case bomb was placed in a busy restaurant, killing two and wounding 136. On Friday 21st July—'Bloody Friday'—they set off nineteen bombs between 2 and 3 p.m. in central Belfast, at bus stations, railway stations, ferry terminals and shopping centres, killing nine people and injuring 130—again, predictably, predominantly women and children.

'Bloody Friday' proved disastrous for the Provisional I.R.A. Reaction everywhere was hostile especially amongst Catholics both in Northern and Southern Ireland. Contributions from the Irish American community, which had risen sharply after 'Bloody Sunday' in January, fell to one quarter. In the wave of revulsion, British troops judged the time ripe to reoccupy a number of hard core districts in which the I.R.A. had been tacitly permitted to operate their own 'government' without interruption for the past year—the 'no-go areas' in Londonderry and Belfast.

The year 1973 was one of the most promising in the history of the Province—a promise sadly unfulfilled. Killings from all causes fell from 467 to 249—a homicide rate which, though vastly greater than in Britain, was only one third of the annual homicide rate in the same year in Detroit. Talks between politicians of all parties in Northern and Southern Ireland and in Great Britain led to a plan for 'power sharing' and a government was elected to resume self-government with a majority of fifty to twenty-eight in the new Stormont Parliament supporting a Cabinet under Mr. Faulkner in which six members were Protestant and five Catholic. The twenty-eight who opposed it were not, of course, Catholics, but extreme 'Loyalist' Protestants.

The new power-sharing Government—a landmark in the history of Ireland—took office in January 1974 but it lived for less than five months. The Protestant backlash, aroused by the I.R.A. killing and the termination of the Protestant Ascendency by direct rule in March 1972, was in full flood. Apart from the formation of the new 'Loyalist' political parties which comprised the twenty-eight opposition members, a gigantic vigilante organization, the Ulster Defence Association (U.D.A.) had been formed. The Orange Order also formed fourteen battalions of Orange Volunteers, organizing and training as a 'Territorial Army' all over the country. Terrorist organizations such as the U.V.F. also gathered many more recruits.

It was not, however, a violent revolt which brought down the power-sharing Government, but a well-organized public utilities strike by Protestant workers in May 1974. This was disowned by the trade union movement which bravely demonstrated against it, but in vain. It was organized on fascist lines, with intimidation of any who attempted to go to work, and its success was largely due to the significant support of the Protestant middle class, who saw in it their one hope of maintaining the Protestant Ascendency. Mr. Faulkner, faced with collapse of the country into chaos, resigned, and direct rule was reinstituted from London. The momentum of the backlash continued, and in elections both for Northern Irish members at Westminster and for a Constitutional Conference in the Province revealed a massive swing away from Mr. Faulkner and other Protestants willing to share power with the Catholics to 'Loyalists' committed to return to total domination. This the British Government was unwilling to accept, and the prospect was bleak.

In 1975, the violence took a new and nastier turn. The

Provisional I.R.A. announced a 'cease fire' which they said they would maintain so long as the British Government carried out its declared intention of releasing all detainees before Christmas 1975—which it did. The number of soldiers and policemen killed in 1975, therefore, fell sharply—but the number of civilians killed was higher than in either 1973 or 1974. Moreover, the pattern had changed. The great majority were killed, not by bombings or gun battles, but by clandestine sectarian and factional murders—that is, by the I.R.A. killing Protestants and the U.V.F. killing Catholics, and also by the rival I.R.A. factions killing each other. The majority of those murdered were Catholics, though it is not possible to say how many of these were killed by Protestants and how many by other Catholics. Both were equally vicious.

It is possible now to draw up a balance sheet of the effectiveness of Provisional I.R.A. terrorism in 1971–75.

Their achievements were considerable. As urban guerrillas, they exercised unchallenged control of large 'no-go areas' in Londonderry and Belfast for a year in 1971–72. Much more important, however, was their success in providing an over-reaction by Stormont which induced the British Government in March 1972 to bring fifty years of discriminatory Protestant rule to an end. This gave them the prestige and the opportunity, had they so chosen, to emerge as a lawful political party to negotiate favourable settlement.

The debit side, however, outweighs their achievements. Having no coherent political philosophy, they were unable to take advantage of the political opportunity they themselves had created. Moreover, by their own excesses (particularly the bombings) they steadily alienated their own Catholic supporters in the North. In January 1972, in areas like the Ardoyne and Andersonstown in Belfast and Creggan and Bogside in Londonderry and in the border area of South Armagh, the Catholic population was solidly behind them—and this probably added up to some ten per cent of the Catholics in Northern Ireland. By 1975, families living in these hard-core areas were becoming exasperated with the continual involvement of their children in the fighting, and it is probable that less than one third, even in these areas, now supported the I.R.A.—that is, only about three per cent of the Northern Ireland Catholic population or one per cent of the

Province as a whole. At the same time, they had caused the over-whelming majority of moderate Catholics to sink their own differences and rally to a united Social Democratic and Labour Party (S.D.L.P.) from the election in 1973 onwards.

The I.R.A. also alienated public opinion in Southern Ireland, and even in the U.S.A., where contributions to the 'welfare' funds which provide a transparent cover for financing and arming the I.R.A. fell to a trickle. Furthermore, they aroused a Protestant backlash with a degree of public support and organization which makes peaceful reunification inconceivable for years to come; partly because the Dublin Army and police force could not possibly control a rebellion by a million thoroughly alienated Protestants absorbed into the Republic against their will, but chiefly because neither the Government in Dublin, nor the people of the South have any desire at present to shatter the peace of the Republic by bringing in the vicious warring factions from the North, whether Protestant or Catholic.

If the British were to get out, as the I.R.A. still go on calling for them to do, this could only result in effective control by Protestant 'Loyalists' wedded to fascist methods, as they demon-strated in 1974. In any ensuing civil war, the highly organized Protestant majority could not fail to win, even though there would be fraternal support for the I.R.A. guerrillas from across the border. In any event, it would be the Catholic minority in the North who would suffer and it is this, presumably, which accounts for the British reluctance to go.

The only 'reunification' which the I.R.A. have achieved has been to bring about unprecedented unity between London and Dublin. This is shared by all political parties—Labour, Con-servative and Liberal in Britain, and Fine Gael, the Irish Labour Party, and Fianna Fail in Ireland—who are united in their opposition to the I.R.A.

Seven years of violence had by 1976 left very few realistic options open for the Northern Irish people. Reunification with the South was effectively ruled out by Dublin itself. No British Parliament was likely to hand over power to an independent Ulster with a fascist government; nor, so long as the Province remained in the United Kingdom, would Parliament agree ever again to use British troops to prop up a mono-sectarian Protestant

3*

Government in Stormont. Only one political option remained: to continue direct rule from London until such time as the Protestant politicians were willing to form a new Stormont Government with proportionate Catholic participation, and with sufficient political support to withstand another fascist-style attempt, like the one in 1974, to bring it down.

In 1976, with no sign of any decline in sectarian killings, a number of influential Unionist and S.D.L.P. politicians appeared, like the majority of their people, to be coming to terms with this equation. One of the stumbling blocks has always been the control of the R.U.C., which many Catholics have regarded as pre-dominantly Protestant-manned, Protestant-controlled and acting with a Protestant bias. The R.U.C. in 1975 itself did much to dispel this image. It formed a highly successful Special Patrol Group, which included a strong team of detectives concentrating on sectarian murders. This led to an encouraging rise in the rate of detection and a build-up of intelligence about both Protestant and Catholic terrorist organizations. Though the number of murders was roughly the same as in 1974, the number of people charged with murder increased by eighty-four per cent. And over sixty per cent of those charged with murder were Protestants. These facts spoke louder than words in discounting the accusation of bias, and in encouraging Catholic politicians to come out openly with what the people themselves had long been saying—that they would rather have the R.U.C. patrolling the streets than the I.R.A. or the U.V.F.

Meanwhile, whether direct rule had to continue for another two years or another ten, the British Government and the British Army were geared for a long haul. In 1972–73, army battalions had been returning for a fourth or fifth time with only five months break between tours. By 1976, the return of the R.U.C. to patrol-ling the streets in more and more districts had enabled the army strength to be so reduced that an infantry battalion could expect to have at least two years at its home base with its families between tours. This would be no strain on the army at all. Service in Ireland had boosted both recruiting and, more importantly, the re-engagement of experienced officers and N.C.O.s. The army could maintain that level for as long as was needed, until the police could complete the process of relieving them in all but the most violent areas, and eventually in those as well.

The end of violence in Northern Ireland was certainly not yet in sight, but at least the options and the likely evolution of events were fairly clear.

Perhaps the last words should go to two Southern Irish politicians—one from each of the two main political parties, both speaking in the United States.

First was Dr. Garret Fitzgerald, Foreign Minister of the Fine Gael Government, speaking in the United Nations on 24th September 1973, following the election of a power-sharing Parliament in the Province:

> We do not seek to impose, or have imposed, on the people of Northern Ireland any solution unacceptable to a majority there. We know that any attempt to impose such a solution could only multiply the bloodshed and the bitterness. It is the *people* of Ireland we seek to unite; the territory of Ireland is nothing without its people, and this unity of the people of Ireland can be secured only in peace and reconciliation with the consent of a majority of the inhabitants of Northern Ireland.

The other quotation is from a speech by Desmond O'Malley, Minister of Justice in the Fianna Fail Government, speaking to the Emerald Association in New York in October 1972:

> The major damage done by the I.R.A. violence is, of course, the damage it does to the prospects for a reconciliation between the two traditions in the North. Another major tragedy is what it is doing to the children and adolescents of the stricken cities of Belfast and Derry, young people whose minds cannot but be seared for a generation to come. The damage to the minds of a generation of young people is almost too terrible to bear thinking about.

6 The Palestinians

Like the I.R.A., the Palestinian terrorists are motivated by nationalism; their grievance is deeply rooted in history, again arising from the settlement of aliens in their country. They are split into various Marxist and nationalist factions which periodically fight each other; and they receive strong financial backing from sympathizers in the rich world—in their case the Arab oil world instead of the U.S.A.

They differ from the I.R.A. in that they are predominantly led by intellectuals, even though some of the rank and file are found from deprived members of the refugee community; they operate all over the world, whereas to date the I.R.A. have operated only in Ireland and in Britain; and the Palestinians have a much more sophisticated organization, using a world network for international hi-jackings and kidnappings to exert political blackmail and to attract publicity for their cause.

Historically, as the Arabs see it, the Jews have no right to Palestine. They left it in A.D. 70, and for eighteen and a half centuries there were very few of them there. The Arabs have been there since before A.D. 700 even though they lived under Turkish rule for about 500 years until 1918. When they co-operated with the British Army in driving out the Turks they were promised, through Lawrence and others, that after liberation they would be able to govern their lands as they wished. This promise cut across the Balfour Declaration of 1917, under which the British Government promised the Jews a National Home in Palestine. In the event, this National Home is located in the coastal plain which is by far the most fertile land in the Levant. In the view of the Palestinian Arabs, the Jews were given the only land worth having, while they were left with the rocky hills and the deserts.

In 1920, around the same time as the partition of Ireland, Britain was given a mandate by the League of Nations to administer the area which now comprises Israel and Jordan. This regularized the *de facto* situation as the British Army which had driven out the Turks was still in occupation. The mandate included a commitment to establish a Jewish National Home in Palestine, though its precise status was left vague.

During the next eighteen years, the British administration did its best to control the flood of Jewish immigrants, initially from Russia and Eastern Europe, increased in the 1920s by the decision of the U.S. Government, beset by the same problem, to limit the quota of Jewish immigration into America. The Nazi persecution of the Jews after 1933 made the pressure intolerable, and by 1938 the proportion of Jews in Palestine had risen to twenty-nine per cent. This had led to growing Arab resistance, which broke out into a full-scale rebellion from 1936 to 1938. This revolt led to the rapid expansion of a Jewish Home Guard in every kibbutz, known as the Haganah.

During the Second World War, the Haganah joined the British in fighting the Nazis, and fought as a Jewish Brigade in the British Army.

After the war, it was clear that the British Labour Government intended to hand over the mandate, but they said that they were only willing to implement a plan to which both Arabs and Jews would agree. As this seemed unlikely, they announced that they would hand over in any case to the United Nations on 15th May 1948.

Meanwhile, an extreme right-wing Jewish terrorist organization, the Irgun Zvai Leumi (I.Z.L.) was demanding that the Jewish National Home should include not only all of Palestine, but also all that is now Jordan. When it was made clear that this was inconceivable, they launched a series of guerrilla attacks on the British Army, which were a matter of considerable embarrassment to the Jewish Agency and the Haganah, which were preparing to become the government and regular army of Israel when the State became independent.

In 1947, the United Nations Special Commission on Palestine (U.N.S.C.O.P.) visited Palestine. They were briefed by the Jewish Agency, but the Arabs boycotted them completely having

made up their minds that, in whatever form the new State of
Israel was created, they would destroy it. They did not, therefore,
wish to tie their hands in any way by taking part in negotiations.

The partition plan was based on ownership of land. By 1947,
individual Jews and the Jewish Agency had purchased most of
the fertile land on the coastal plain from Arab landowners and the
author (who was serving with the British Army in Palestine at the
time) recalls three maps, one showing irrigated, cultivated land, a
second showing land owned by Jews and the third showing the
United Nations' partition plan. The three were very nearly
identical.

The proposed State of Israel, however, had a hopelessly unrealistic shape as a result of this. It was in places less than twelve
miles wide between the frontier with Jordan and the sea. During
the final months before partition, when these frontiers were
known, there were repeated terrorist incidents by both sides,
resulting in 150,000 Arab refugees fleeing across the frontier.
During those months, also, the armies of Syria, Jordan and
Egypt prepared to invade the new State as soon as the British
Army had gone, and the Haganah prepared to defend it.

No one gave the Haganah much chance, but the Arabs, after
some initial penetration, were driven back and the frontiers of
Israel were straightened out and widened before the United
Nations managed to secure an armistice in April 1949. By this
time, the number of Arab refugees had risen to 900,000.

In 1954, after President Nasser came to power in Egypt, Arab
guerrillas intensified raids into Israel, chiefly from the Gaza strip.
This led to the Americans, British and French jointly deciding
not to supply arms to Egypt unless these attacks were discon-
tinued. Egypt promptly signed an arms deal with Russia. The
U.S.A. retaliated by reversing their decision to finance the Aswan
Dam through the World Bank. The Egyptians thereupon
nationalized the Suez Canal and this, together with the Fedayeen
raids, led to the Suez War in 1956, when the Israeli Army occupied
the Sinai Peninsula from which they withdrew reluctantly under
American pressure on the promise that it would be policed by a
United Nations Force.

During the next ten years, guerrilla attacks intensified, and from
1965 an increasing number of Palestinian guerrillas were taking

part. The Israelis retaliated with raids into Jordan. The Syrians then began to bombard agricultural settlements overlooked by the Golan Heights. Israel threatened to invade Syria, and the Egyptians, hoping to take the pressure off Syria, moved a large army into Sinai Desert, ordering the United Nations Forces to leave. Amongst the places they occupied was Sharm-el-Sheikh, which overlooks the narrow Straits of Tiran. Nasser announced that the Straits would be closed, thereby cutting off Israel's only access to the Indian Ocean through the Gulf of Akaba. Since the Suez Canal was already closed to her, Israel announced that any interference with shipping entering the Gulf of Akaba would be taken as an act of war.

The Israelis invaded on three fronts in June 1967, and within six days they had driven the Syrians off the Golan Heights, the Jordanians out of Jerusalem and back to the east bank of the Jordan River, and the Egyptians across the Suez Canal. The number of Arab refugees swelled to one and a half million.

The Arabs had now lost every square yard of Palestine and a good deal more. The occupied territories provided a buffer against every Palestinian guerrilla base except in Lebanon.

It was this which led the Palestinian guerrillas to turn their activities from Israel to the rest of the world. During the next few years, various factions split from each other, though all acknowledged to some extent the authority of the Palestine Liberation Organization (P.L.O.). The main guerrilla movements were as follows.

Al Fatah, originally formed from the Muslim brotherhood in 1956, but not really effective until 1968, was the largest movement, and the most moderate. It was led by Yasser Arafat who was also President of the P.L.O. Its strength is 7,000–9,000.

The Black September Organization (B.S.O.) was a violent off-shoot of Al Fatah, formed after the decimation of the Arab guerrillas in Jordan in September 1970, as described below.

The Popular Front for the Liberation of Palestine (P.F.L.P.) is a Marxist movement formed in 1968 by Dr. George Habbash. It was supported by Iraq and other radical Arab states, and was responsible for most of the spectacular hi-jackings during the years 1968 to 1972. Its strength is about 500.

The Popular Democratic Front for the Liberation of Palestine

(P.D.F.L.P.), led by Naif Hawatmeh, is an extreme Marxist movement which broke away from the P.F.L.P. and rejects all Arab governments, traditional or otherwise, declaring its intention of replacing them all with people's democracies.

Saiqa is a large group over 2,000 strong and is tightly controlled by the Government of Syria, where it is based. It has from time to time played a big part in the civil war in Lebanon.

These movements have a combined strength of about 12,000, of whom seventy per cent are based in Lebanon.

The first Palestinian hi-jacking was in July 1968, by the P.F.L.P. Till then, hi-jacking had been largely confined to Cuba and the U.S.A. The P.F.L.P. hi-jacked an El Al aircraft and diverted it to Algeria. This was one of the few occasions on which the Israelis gave way to political blackmail, and they agreed to an Algerian request to release sixteen Arab prisoners. After two more attacks on El Al aircraft, the Israelis tightened up their pre-cautions, installing locked bullet-proofed cockpit doors and armed sky marshals. P.F.L.P. therefore switched their attacks to other aircraft and on 29th August 1969 Leila Khaled led a P.F.L.P. team which hi-jacked a TWA 707 to Damascus.

During the next year, a number of Palestinian terrorists were arrested and held in custody after attacks in Greece, Switzerland and West Germany. With a view to getting these released, the P.F.L.P. attempted to hi-jack three more aircraft in September 1970. One of these misfired, and Leila Khaled, as described earlier, was handed over to the British police by the crew of an aircraft which made a forced landing in London. The P.F.L.P. then hi-jacked a British aircraft. They seized a disused air field, Dawson's Field, in Jordan, and three aircraft were gathered there on the ground—one American, one British and one Swiss, carrying a total of over 400 passengers. After some days of negotiations, all the hostages were released in exchange for the release of seven Palestinian terrorists from Germany, Switzerland and Britain, though the aircraft were blown up.

This incident caused a wave of revulsion all over the world. King Hussein of Jordan, after the hostages were released, seized the opportunity of driving the Palestinian guerrillas out of his country, which they were openly threatening to take over. In the climate of feeling after Dawson's Field, no Arab country made any serious attempt to help the guerrillas, large numbers of whom were killed. Most of those who escaped moved into Syria and Lebanon.

It was in mourning for this defeat that a group of young militants from Al Fatah formed the Black September Organization. During the next year, the B.S.O. and P.F.L.P. concentrated their attacks mainly against Jordanian aircraft, but the Jordanians, like the Israelis, had instituted effective precautions, and the guerrillas had little success. In February 1972, they hi-jacked a Lufthansa aircraft and the West German Government paid a record ransom of $5 million. Then on 9th May 1972 a group of P.F.L.P. terrorists attempting to hi-jack a Sabena aircraft on the ground at Lod Airport near Tel Aviv were attacked and captured by Israeli security guards. In revenge for this, three Japanese terrorists massacred twenty-four passengers at this same airport on 30th May 1972.

The story of this massacre illustrates the international nature of P.F.L.P.'s. operations. The three Japanese, all graduates, were initially recruited into an extreme revolutionary group in Japan, the United Red Army. As it was difficult to train with live ammunition in Japan, they went to North Korea for training. Here they were recruited by the P.F.L.P. and moved to a refugee camp in Lebanon for final training and briefing. From there they went to Frankfurt, where they were equipped with false papers, and then to Rome where they each collected a suitcase containing Czech weapons and ammunition. These suitcases were loaded as passenger baggage without search into the hold of an Air France aircraft bound for Lod Airport. On arrival, they opened their suitcases in the baggage lobby and opened fire indiscriminately, killing twenty-four people, mainly Puerto Rican Christian pilgrims on their way to Bethlehem and Jerusalem, and wounding seventy-two others. Two of the Japanese were killed by their own fire, and the third was captured. At his trial in Israel he made a long statement, some of which is revealing:

Revolutionary warfare is warfare for justice, which I define as creating a society with no class struggle. War involves killing and destruction. We cannot limit warfare to the destruction of buildings. We believe that the killing of human beings is inevitable . . . The Arab world lacks spiritual fervour, so we felt that through this attempt we could probably stir up the Arab world.

On 5th September 1972, at the Munich Olympics, eight Palestinian terrorists (B.S.O.) kidnapped eleven Israeli Olympic athletes with the primary purpose of gaining publicity. All the athletes were killed, and five of the terrorists, the other three being captured by the West Germans, but later released in the face of another hi-jacking operation. The publicity achieved at Munich, however, was spectacular, and it is estimated that 500 million people watched the event on television all over the world. Though the overwhelming majority will have been revolted by it, many will have learned of the Palestinian cause for the first time, and a tiny percentage will have had some sympathy with it. A tiny percentage of 500 million is still a lot of people, so the operation must be regarded as having achieved its aim.

Another successful kidnapping occurred a year later when three hostages were taken off a train in Austria. The Palestinians released the hostages in exchange for Chancellor Kreisky of Austria agreeing to close the Schonau Transit Camp for Jewish refugees on their way from Russia to Israel. This was the first time that a government had actually changed its policy, as opposed to releasing prisoners, in the face of political blackmail, and the Israeli Prime Minister, Mrs. Golda Meir, visited a number of capitals trying to enlist international support to get the decision reversed.

Two weeks later, on 6th October 1973, the Egyptians and Syrians invaded the Sinai Desert and the Golan Heights. It now seems likely that the Austrian kidnapping was deliberately designed to divert Israeli attention from the build-up for the war, and this theory is supported by the fact that the terrorists were from Saiqa, the movement which is most closely controlled by the Syrian Government.

During that war, in which the Arabs lived down some of their earlier humiliations, they also learned to use the oil weapon. The way was led by King Feisal of Saudi Arabia, who first reduced the delivery of oil and then, along with the other OPEC countries, quadrupled the price.

The oil weapon has now proved itself incomparably more effective than terrorism, and the Arab Governments are showing a growing disillusion with the Palestinian terrorists. This was demonstrated soon after the October War, in December 1973, when terrorists killed thirty-three airline passengers in Rome and Athens and were refused permission to land by every Arab country, including Libya, which physically blocked the runways to prevent them from doing so. Again in February 1974, a mixed group of Palestinians and Japanese hi-jacked a ferry after an abortive attempt to blow up an oil refinery on an island off Singapore. The Singapore police held the ferry under armed surveillance and the P.F.L.P. used their world-wide network to rescue the terrorists, occupying the Japanese Embassy in Kuwait and holding members of the staff as hostages. The Japanese agreed to provide an aircraft to pick up the terrorists in Singapore and fly them to Kuwait, where the Government again initially refused them permission to land, but gave way in the face of a threat to kill the Embassy staff.

In 1974–75, therefore, the terrorists once more switched their main effort to Israel itself. They suffered very heavy casualties, very few of the terrorists getting out alive, and they sacrificed much sympathy by, for example, killing twenty school-children in Ma'alot in May 1974. The Israelis, however, made the serious error of throwing away world sympathy by launching air attacks on refugee camps alleged to contain guerrilla bases in Lebanon, and the world press was filled with pictures of dead and wounded Arab women and children as gruesome as those of the Israeli children at Ma'alot.

In December 1975 the Palestinians struck out in a fresh direction by attacking the Arab oil states themselves in one of the most bizarre of all terrorist operations—the kidnapping of eleven Oil Ministers at the OPEC meeting in Vienna. In the face of threats of death to two of these, the Ministers from Saudi Arabia and Kuwait, they were all flown to Algiers where both the hostages and the kidnappers were released. Various statements were read out over radio and television, but as this was known to be done under duress it can have had little effect. In fact, the only aim of the operation appears to have been publicity, and this publicity is unlikely to have done the Palestinian cause much good on the eve of an important U.N. debate. Nor did their humiliation at Entebbe in July 1976, when more than 100 Israeli hostages held by Palestinian and German hi-jackers were rescued in a daring Israeli commando raid.

As in the case of the I.R.A., the achievements of the Palestinian terrorists have been considerable in the short term, but appear to be counter-productive in the long term. It has so alienated the rest of the world that probably nothing could have saved the movement but the oil weapon. Operations like the kidnapping of the OPEC Ministers seem to risk alienating the very Arab Governments which operate that weapon. As it is, the Arabs have progressively lost more and more of Palestine until they have none of it left. It remains to be seen whether the Arab Governments will be able and willing to continue to use the oil weapon to get at least some of Palestine back, which the use of terrorism has signally failed to do.

7 The Terrorist International

The OPEC kidnapping and the Entebbe hi-jack, like the Lod Airport massacre in May 1972, again demonstrated the willingness of the Palestinians to employ members of other international terrorist movements. At Vienna, the leader was reputed to be a Latin American (using the name of Carlos) wanted for offences in Paris and elsewhere, and he shot one of the three people killed. The other two were shot by a West German girl who had earlier been imprisoned for offences with the Baader-Meinhof gang and had been set free as part of the political blackmail paid for the release of Peter Lorenz, when he was kidnapped in West Berlin.

These international terrorist movements are initially formed by people who seek revolutionary change inside their own countries but become frustrated by the inability of other Marxist movements, whether orthodox or extreme, to bring it about by political or industrial action. They believe that such movements must fail because the overwhelming majority of people do not want their lives to be disrupted by revolutionary change. They therefore aim to bring their society into such a state of chaos that the people will cease to believe that the existing system can maintain an orderly life for them in any case. Most of them would subscribe to the philosophy of 'Situationism'. Devotees of this philosophy believe that the whole pattern of civilized life, as most people understand it, is artificial and unnatural and that if people can be made to realize this they will begin spontaneously to take their lives into their own hands without regard for the remainder of the community or its laws, 'opting out' as some squatters do when they set up communes in derelict houses, existing without money by scavenging and theft. The first stage is for enough people to do this for chaos to spread and confidence to be undermined, so that more and more people do it in desperation at the inability of society to provide for their needs. The community would crumble into chaos, at first gradually, and then accelerating towards a galloping collapse.

It is fruitless to look for logic in this plan. If civilized society collapsed there would very soon be nothing to scavenge. Since many countries are now so overpopulated that they could not grow enough food to survive at all without exports and imports, the plan would clearly sentence a very large number of people to death. Those who genuinely believe in it can only be described as mad, and this is the clear impression which emerges from a reading of the testimony of the Japanese terrorist who survived the Lod massacre. Others, no doubt, do realize that, at a fairly early stage of the crumble towards chaos, some kind of authoritarian leadership would seize control and a frightened public would rally to it. This would be either an orthodox communist party or, more likely, some kind of fascist or military organization. This may be what the Situationist wants in his heart, either from a form of masochism, or because this is what he actually wants all the time and believes that the spectre of collapse into the jungle will alarm people into clustering round any plausible Queen Ant and begging to be regimented.

The more extreme Situationists believe that it is necessary for collapse to be international for two reasons: firstly because, otherwise, a neighbouring country, still stable, will step in and the people will welcome it; and secondly that this can be insured against best by arranging for the accelerating collapse in one country to shake the stability of the other countries which trade with it, so that none are in the position to perform the rescue.

This dangerous form of madness seems to be a product, not of poverty, but of affluence and higher education. Those who develop it invariably claim to be acting on behalf of the deprived sectors of the community and some of them try deliberately to become deprived themselves, living 'on the run' in conditions of squalor, as did the members of the Angry Brigade in Britain and the Symbionese Liberation Army in the U.S.A. (It is significant, however, that the very few violent movements which are recruited from genuinely deprived people, such as the I.R.A. and U.V.F., are neither Situationist nor international in their operations.) The overwhelming majority of members of the international terrorist movements, including all but a proportion of the rank and file of the Palestinian terrorist groups, come from middle-class families and most of them have received more than average education. Though some of the middle-class Palestinian guerrillas will have suffered the indignity of being refugees, very few international terrorists have known real want and deprivation as children; nor have they been brought up in the harsh school of a poor industrial neighbourhood, where the boys (and girls) settle their quarrels with fists, and later broken bottles, rather than with barbed words. Most terrorists have no connection with the 'working class' they claim to represent, and are disowned by them.

Amongst the first in the field were the American Weathermen, a violent off-shoot from the Students for a Democratic Society. All the convicted members of the Angry Brigade had been to university. The members of the Baader-Meinhof gang (or Red Army Fraction) were recruited from a sports-car set and, unlike some, used the proceeds from bank robberies to maintain that style of life. About thirty Tupamaros guarded the British Ambassador, Sir Geoffrey Jackson, during his eight-month captivity, but very few of these were manual workers, probably only one—the others were all university students or graduates. So were the three Japanese terrorists who carried out the Lod Airport massacre. The Symbionese Liberation Army (S.L.A.) was begun by a group of radical students at Berkeley, mainly women. Though they recruited four convicts, two black and two white, into their ranks (their title indicated a 'symbiosis' or fusion between the intellectuals and the deprived), the intellectuals remained always in a majority and, despite public reference to one of the black convicts as leader, they always directed the movement.

The S.L.A. illustrates an interesting tendency amongst nearly all intellectual revolutionaries, whether terrorist or not, to seek an inverted respectability by getting as near as possible to being 'working-class'. One manifestation of this is the quest, in the commune, for the very squalor from which most manual workers and their families have long since broken out. Another manifestation is the yearning to recruit deprived (and, in America, black) people into their movements. Sadly, such recruits are usually rootless and inadequate, unable to cope with ordinary life, and still less with the hardships of being a revolutionary, so that what is left of their lives is smashed beyond hope of recovery.

Why do such affluent children turn to violence? Why does this fringe of university students and graduates, equipped to contribute so much to the community, try to destroy it? The proportion who do so is very small, but they can do much damage and cause much misery to the people least equipped to withstand it.

It is a great mistake to confuse peaceful protest with destruction and violence. Protest is healthy and essential. Societies tend to adapt too slowly to changing conditions because those with power and authority, who could and should make the changes, have a natural desire to keep the *status quo* because they themselves are satisfied and fulfilled. Two passages are worth quoting from Norman Cantor's excellent book *The Age of Protest* (London, Allen & Unwin, 1970):

> Protest in the twentieth century has led to social change. Revolution has been the road to chaos, civil war and new tyranny.
>
> The leadership of twentieth-century protest movements almost invariably consisted of particularly sensitive and energetic members of the middle class who had sufficient familiarity with the power elite not to fear them greatly, sufficient leisure to engage in dissident activities and sufficient education and political experience to know where and how the power elite was most vulnerable.

and one from Eric Ashby's and Mary Anderson's *The Rise of the Student Estate* (London, Macmillan, 1970):

> . . . no changes in the structure of society, good or bad, peaceful or ugly, from Galilee to Cuba, have occurred without pioneers labelled as lunatics . . . It would be a dull conscience which was not stirred by demonstrations to call attention to the homeless, the hungry and the victims of oppression. It is not the strategy of student protest which is itself evil, it is the way the strategy is manipulated by some student groups for ignoble ends, or directed into the paths of violence.

About ten per cent of British university students can be described as 'protestors'. They are willing to be called out on demonstrations to protest against what they feel to be injustices and to apply pressure upon those in authority—sometimes with a degree of disruption, but seldom with destruction or violence—to persuade them to do something about it. About one per cent can be described as politically extreme and have politics which are revolutionary rather than reformist. It is the political extremists who usually provide the leadership for the protestors, selecting the issues on which they think people will turn out to demonstrate. These issues may be selected in good faith, in which case the demonstration can be taken at its face value. On the other hand, they may be selected as a pretext for a confrontation, unknown to the majority of the protestors, whose real aim is to poison the relationship of their community with the authorities or with the police—manipulating the genuine feelings of the protestors for what Ashby and Anderson describe as 'ignoble ends'.

So typically, in a university of 5,000, about 500 is a fair average of the number who will turn out to protest, of whom about fifty are members of extreme political movements. The number of these, however, who will want to *initiate* violence for political purposes is unlikely to be more than about four or five, and their violence would only take the form of hitting people or throwing things. The number likely to use lethal violence is very small indeed. According to an intelligence source in West Germany, there are probably only sixty to eighty people in that country who would deliberately kill with their own hands for political ends and perhaps another 600 who would aid and abet them in that killing by driving cars, acting as look-outs, etc. Within German universities there may perhaps be another 2,000–3,000 who express public sympathy to the extent of justifying the killing in demonstrations in favour of the Baader-Meinhof gang. A similar source suggested that the numbers in Britain are probably very similar to these.

Thus, a fair assessment in British universities is that one in ten are protestors, one in a hundred are politically extreme, and one in a thousand are politically violent without being lethal. In the country as a whole (excluding Northern Ireland) only about one in a million would choose to kill for political aims. Few, if any, of these could be described as 'working-class'.

But why? Why do middle-class children, even in these tiny

proportions, become politically extreme or violent or even lethal?

A cynic would say that it is easier for a middle-class boy or girl to play with political extremism or violence than for those who lack his background and education. He has a number of safety-nets into which he can fall. He knows that, if he wants to get a job, he will be able to do so. Even if it is not a white collar one, he will be paid just as much. With his intelligence and education he knows that he will be able to play the social security system to his benefit, and there will have been a branch of the Claimants' Union at his university to teach him how. He also knows at the back of his mind that, if all goes wrong or if he tires of revolution, a loving family will welcome him back and will have the means to salvage his life.

It would be a mistake, however, to discount the genuine ideological motivation which he may have. His disquiet with the injustices of a 'free society' is usually sincere. He rejects the consumer society and wants to opt out of it but he still has the normal human desire for achievement. Having opted out of the rat-race, he still wants to call a tune to which others will dance. He finds that at university there are people who will dance to his tune—the 'protestors'.

On the other hand, one of the less attractive features about the intellectual revolutionary, whether violent or not, is his contempt for the mass of the people. From reading Marcuse and others, he acquires the belief that ordinary people have been conned, first at school and then by the media, into accepting society as it is. The 'working class', lulled by a rising standard of living and by 'repressive tolerance', bemused by the 'spectacle' of the bread and circuses of an artificial society, has ceased to be revolutionary material. It does not occur to him that working men are less gullible about swallowing what is fed to them by the media than he is himself about swallowing what is fed to him by revolutionary theorists. His reading, and his discussions with those of like mind at university, convince him that he knows what is good for the proletariat better than the proletariat itself. It is not surprising that this arrogant assumption earns him little respect from the 'working class'.

The tragedy is that this revolutionary indoctrination, which might otherwise be harmless or even beneficial in the development of a young idealist, can pervert the idealism and generosity of some of its victims so that a hard shell forms around them, further hardened by the rejection they experience from those whom they wish to liberate. This has been movingly described by Sir Geoffrey Jackson in his account of his kidnapping by intellectual terrorists in his book *People's Prison* (London, Faber & Faber, 1973). Cooped up with his hooded guards in a tiny cellar separated from them only by a piece of pig netting, he managed to get through to at least some of those who were still young enough for the human spirit not to have withered entirely within them. He did this by making them laugh but, sadly, the entry of another guard or some kind of alarm would often break the spell, and the human being would vanish once again into the shell. He came to the conclusion that, however young, once they had killed a man they were probably committed beyond hope of cure.

There seems to be no instance in history of an *established* liberal pluralist society being overthrown by a Marxist or anarchist revolution. Many, however, have been taken over by right-wing or military *coups d'état*. Crane Brinton, in his *Anatomy of Revolution* (New York, Vintage, 1957) describes how the process always seems to begin with an autocratic regime. This is ousted by a frustrated middle-class movement which contains both 'moderates' and 'extremists'. The moderates are committed to liberal democracy and to the dismantling of the apparatus of repression. Before they can establish anything stable in its place the extremists seize the chance to oust the moderates and seize power themselves. The extremists then find that, since their system cannot accommodate dissent, they can only enforce discipline by State terror. This leads either to a dictatorship of the left or a reaction throwing up a dictatorship of the right. This pattern can be clearly discerned in the French Revolution and the Russian Revolution, and the early stages of it were certainly apparent in Portugal in 1974–75.

There is an alternative—the 'constitutional' road to a one-party Marxist state. This has never quite been achieved anywhere, though it was close to success in President Allende's Chile. It is certainly conceivable in France and Italy, where the orthodox communists and left-wing socialists could gain a majority with a promise of continuing parliamentary democracy, and then adjust the electoral process to produce the ninety-nine per cent votes which are a standard feature in the Soviet Union and other Marxist states. It is, however, unlikely in any of the other established parliamentary democracies, such as West Germany, the Benelux countries, the U.S.A., Australia, New Zealand or Great Britain. In these countries, most of the revolutionaries in any case reject the constitutional road as being likely to produce an 'alternative bureaucracy' which would repress their dissent as ruthlessly as it is repressed in Russia. They accept that there is no 'revolutionary situation' in these countries at present, and that they must therefore go through a 'fascist stage first'. Perhaps unconsciously, therefore, they are subscribing to Crane Brinton's theory, and are anxious to force their governments to adopt measures so repressive that they will arouse discontent amongst liberally-minded people, thereby putting the Crane Brinton process into operation.

For this purpose they draw upon the philosophy of Carlos Marighela, expounded in his *Mini-manual of the Urban Guerrilla*, which can best be read in his *For the Liberation of Brazil* (London, Penguin, 1971). Marighela says that the urban guerrilla must create a situation in which the government has no option but to use repressive measures. Liberal forms of law are made unworkable by intimidating witnesses and juries, so that more arbitrary forms of law have to be substituted. Disruption, damage and loss of life reach a scale which compels the government to introduce curfews, roadblocks, searches and mass arrests. This harassment starts the process of discontent with the government. It is continued by bombing which destroys places of work and deters investment, so that unemployment is increased. To use Marighela's own words, the aim is to make life 'unbearable' for ordinary people, and to 'transform a political situation into a military situation'. In this 'climate of collapse' it is possible that the people may call for a popular front government in which the political wing of the guerrillas will have a part. This, in effect, enters the Crane Brinton process at the second stage. In practice, however, the chaos brought about by the urban guerrillas more often provokes a military *coup d'état*, and the Crane Brinton process can then begin at the first stage.

This internal process can be accelerated by international action in several ways. Urban guerrillas from other countries looking for a suitable stage for international operations for their own purposes, are welcomed by indigenous guerrilla movements as assisting in the provocation of repressive measures and the move towards a climate of collapse. This accounts for the support by some extreme Marxist movements for bombing operations by the Provisional I.R.A. in England; also for the support by indigenous movements of Palestinian terrorist operations worldwide; and for the co-operation of guerrilla movements in various Latin American countries. From the other direction, the guerrillas may hope to provoke intervention by foreign governments in support of the *status quo*. It is probable that some Tupamaros hoped for overt intervention by Brazil, which would undoubtedly have evoked a hostile response from liberal elements in Uruguay.

Foreign intervention, direct or indirect, in internal war has now become a common means whereby one nation exercises pressure on another or tries to bring about the kind of government which it would like to see—things which in past centuries would have been done by direct military action or diplomacy. The U.S.A., Russia and China all helped the side they wanted to win in Indo-China in the 1960s. Even more countries interfered in Angola in 1976— Russia, Cuba, the U.S.A., South Africa, Zambia and Zaire. The foreign country may sometimes take such a positive initiative that it could be described as sponsoring an internal conflict which might otherwise not have occurred. This, however, is much less common than exploiting an existing conflict of trying to influence its out-come. This may take the form of sending combat units, such as the Americans sent to Vietnam and Cuba sent to Angola; or specialists such as helicopter pilots; or advisers. Sometimes the aid consists mainly of money, weapons and supplies, but it almost invariably includes help with propaganda, both to exacerbate the conflict inside the country and to rally support outside it.

International urban guerrillas, however, rely more on fraternal aid from sympathetic groups in the target country than they do on governments. These sympathetic groups may be found from amongst immigrant communities, such as Arab students or workers in European countries; or they may consist of indigenous groups, such as the International Marxist Group which has provided propaganda support for I.R.A. operations in England.

When operating in a foreign country, some of the things which international terrorists need are more safely acquired inside the target country than smuggled across its frontier—for example, guns, ammunition, explosives and stolen cars with false number plates. There are, however, exceptions. When Dolours Price tried to blow up Scotland Yard and the Old Bailey in London in March 1973, she brought over her team of eleven in four cars, with the explosives hidden inside them, by the car ferry from Ireland. This, however, is rare, and most I.R.A. teams operating in England have obtained their materials, and most of their men, from amongst the Irish community in London and the Midlands. In any event, international terrorists will need a 'safe house' within the country from which to work. For operations requiring only guns or small 'shopping-bag' bombs, a small flat or bed-sitting room may suffice. For operations requiring large car-bombs, a garage or store is more likely to be used.

International terrorism of this kind is likely to increase because, in the short term at least, it seems to the terrorists to pay, in terms of political blackmail, ransoms and publicity. Political blackmail has succeeded, not only in releasing convicted prisoners, but in persuading governments to change their policy, as the Austrian Government did in September 1973 when it closed the Schonau Transit Camp for Russian Jews on the way to Israel. Enormous ransoms have been obtained, particularly in Latin America. One group in Argentina claimed to have taken US $30 million in 1973 alone. Such huge sums inevitably attract criminal gangs, which are happy to work behind the cover of a political movement in exchange for providing the professional services and communications of the criminal network. Publicity has been fantastic. Just as the kidnapping at the 1972 Munich Olympics attracted huge television audiences all over the world, there must have been few countries in which the kidnapping of the OPEC Oil Ministers in Vienna in 1975 was not headline news. This, indeed, appears to have been its sole aim.

Another motivation of some terrorists is a psychological one, a desire to express hate and revenge, to smash, to kill and to disrupt—or simply to 'feel big'. Feeling big may be achieved by a hoax call, the caller watching gleefully from a window while the police clear the streets. Nothing, however, makes a terrorist feel so big as to have ministers and senior police officers negotiating with him in front of television cameras and conceding to his demands.

Whatever its short-term satisfactions, however, terrorism does not seem to pay in the long term, and there are encouraging signs that some at least of the terrorist movements may be beginning to realize this. The Protestants in Northern Ireland can see that the U.W.C. strike in 1974 achieved more than all the terrorism of the U.V.F. By a self-imposed cease fire in 1975, the Provisional I.R.A. got all their detainees released. Even the Palestinians attempted fewer terrorist operations in 1974–75 than in previous years, and the other Arab governments showed markedly less sympathy for them; the oil weapon was more effective and terrorism prejudiced it.

Nevertheless, the increasing vulnerability of modern society does attract terrorism. International terrorists, who are worldly wise, find it easy to travel. Ideas for terrorist activities travel too, not only in the underground press, but by ordinary news reporting of events. If 500 million people learned about what happened at Munich in 1972, they will have included a number, even if a very small proportion, who might like to use similar methods themselves.

Ultimately, terrorism can be defeated only if it can be seen not to pay, both in the long term and the short term. This is primarily a task for good police work, supported by cool and determined government, and by a co-operative public, and the media have a vital part to play. Meanwhile, until terrorism is defeated, the public must be protected against it, and in such a way that the reaction does not do more damage than the terrorist acts themselves.

8   Protection against terrorism

Can terrorism be eradicated? Obviously not completely, any more than wasps, rats or snakes can be eradicated completely. Can it be defeated? It can, in the sense of making it not pay. Can society be protected against it? Again, not completely. So long as there are wasps and snakes, some people will be stung and bitten. The hazard of terrorism can, however, be kept down to the level of other hazards. The problem is to do this without excessive disruption to daily life, and without too much diversion of resources from more constructive activities; and especially without so restricting civil liberties that society is more damaged by repression than by the terrorism itself.

Society has to protect its citizens against two separate threats: firstly the threat of death and mutilation; secondly, the denial of freedom of choice at gunpoint—that is, the coercion of authorities or individuals into doing things, or permitting things, against their will.

Leaders of tribes and states and their agents have been the targets of the political terrorist since the dawn of civilization, but they are no longer the only targets, or even the prime targets. The great majority of those killed in Northern Ireland have been ordinary citizens. Of the fifty people killed in England for political aims in 1973–75, twelve were soldiers off duty (one of them a girl recruit), but they were picked casually and none of them were officers. Another was a police constable on duty; only one was selected personally, and he was a writer (Ross McWhirter, editor of the *Guinness Book of Records*) who had recommended strong action against terrorists, and was presumably killed to deter others from doing so. All the other thirty-six were indiscriminate victims who happened to be in the pub or other place selected for the terrorist attack. One hundred per cent protection of individuals against this type of attack is clearly impossible. The aim must be to make the terrorists themselves realize that it does not pay.

The price which the English public has paid, however, in terms of disruption, inconvenience, diversion of resources and denial of freedom of choice has been a heavy one, and this must itself be of encouragement to the terrorists. This encouragement, however, has been outweighed by the realization that each incident has further alienated public opinion worldwide, and greatly increased public support for the police.

The more the public knows about terrorists and how they work, the better they will be able to co-operate with the police in protecting themselves and, above all, in assisting in a high rate of arrest and conviction which is the real deterrent. This is where books such as George Styles' *Bombs Have No Pity* (London, William Luscombe, 1975) and *People's Prison* by Geoffrey Jackson can be of tremendous help.

George Styles, who won the George Cross for dealing with bombs in Northern Ireland, stresses that there are many more people involved in a bomb operation than those who actually lay the bomb and who usually get caught. First there is the designer, a back-room boy far too valuable to risk on the operation itself. He also probably has a hand in the acquisition of the explosives, detonators and firing mechanisms. All of these, again, involve a number of people who steal or smuggle these items from different places, and each of them can give a clue to people who are sharp-eyed and aware, and give the police a lead into the system. Next in line is the man who assembles the bomb and its container; his particular skill is in camouflage, so that it looks like an innocuous hold-all or shopping bag. Then there is the electrician, who assembles the firing circuit and, in a sophisticated bomb, inserts some anti-handling device; his skills lie not only in the un-detectability and effectiveness of his circuit, but also in arranging a simple and foolproof means of arming it or putting it into operation such as can be done by the relatively unskilled bomb layer in a tense situation without arousing suspicion.

As important as the designer is the bomb officer, who is in charge of the operation as a whole, and co-ordinates the activities of the technical experts, the layers and their auxiliaries, including the timing of any warning which may be given. These include one

4

or two bomb layers with a driver; they have to know the exact route, where to park and how to get away, and precisely what time to place the bomb. They will be supported by pre-positioned look-outs who signal them if all is clear, and possibly also gunmen, either to clear a building if the aim is only the destruction of property, or, if necessary, to protect the bomb layers. Then there may be someone to telephone a message at a prearranged time, or on receipt of a signal. It was the timing of this call which led to the heavy casualties in the Birmingham pub bombs in November 1974 —casualties which the I.R.A. realize were counterproductive to their cause.

A great many of these activities, not just the placing of the bomb, are liable to be seen by the public if they know what to look for. In particular, they may spot something which indicates the location of the 'safe house' from which the terrorists are mounting the operation. This can be the most valuable intelligence of all.

Kidnapping is the form of political terrorism most closely linked to ordinary crime—that is, to crime for personal gain rather than for political dividends. Political terrorists may need the professional services of criminal gangs to provide such things as stolen cars with false number plates, 'safe houses' and communications networks. The criminal gangs are drawn by the prospect of large ransoms and by the advantages of operating behind the cover of a political group whose members may turn over fast between leaving university and settling down to a more normal life, and to whom the police therefore have few leads. The characteristics of a kidnapping for political aims and one for criminal gain are very similar.

Kidnappings in Britain have been mercifully rare. Mr. and Mrs. Matthews were kidnapped in Balcombe Street by a gang of gunmen whose immediate motive was to escape arrest rather than obtain political dividends. In Italy, kidnappings for criminal gain greatly outnumber those for political aims, but elsewhere, as in the case of Dr. Herrema in the Republic of Ireland, most of them do have a political flavour. The commonest victims are diplomats (primarily for political blackmail) or business executives (primarily for ransom, though not in the case of Dr. Herrema).

An analysis of thirty-five major political kidnappings between

January 1968 and June 1973 showed that sixty per cent of the victims were abducted while driving between home and work, and another thirty per cent from home—usually while coming out of the door to go to work. Only five per cent were taken from their place of work, and the other five per cent fell into no particular category.

Sir Geoffrey Jackson, British Ambassador in Uruguay in 1971, was one of those kidnapped from his car on the way to work. He began to sense, as early as March 1970, that he was a likely target for kidnapping by the Tupamaros. During that month there were six major political kidnappings in Latin America—of a Russian, three Americans, a Japanese and a West German. All were diplomats and the West German (the Ambassador in Guatemala) was killed. Kidnappings continued in April and May, so Jackson flew to London in June, with his wife, to discuss the situation with the British Foreign Office. They all three agreed that, if he were kidnapped, they would immediately declare that there would be no giving way to blackmail or to demands for ransom.

For the next six months, Jackson became increasingly aware that he was being watched with a view to a kidnap. Almost every day a young student-aged 'family', father, mother and baby, sat down for a picnic in the park immediately opposite his home. The 'family' changed, but the pattern was always the same. He also saw a boy and a girl canoodling outside the entrance when he arrived at the Embassy, but he noticed that their attention was not on each other but on him. Their scooter was parked nearby and a check on its number plate traced it to a university student of known Tupamaro sympathies. His car was also regularly shadowed on its way between his residence and the Embassy by a scooter which, although ridden by a different boy and girl, was always the same one with the same number plates. He also became aware of 'dummy runs' by cars and trucks, again often the same ones, cutting in on his official car, clearly aiming to select a suitable site for an ambush. He began to recognize faces which he was to see again when he was kidnapped.

The British Embassy was in the old business centre of Montevideo where the streets were so narrow and congested that a getaway after a kidnap would be very difficult. He therefore judged that an attempt would be much likelier on the wide and often empty streets in the suburbs. He therefore developed a series of alternative routes and varied his timings through the suburbs. The Tupamaros then realized that it would be difficult to catch him anywhere outside the old city so they in fact planned their kidnap *in* the old city close to the Embassy because this was the one place through which he had no choice but to travel. This involved them in an elaborately co-ordinated operation which was expensive in manpower and vehicles, for they had to block every junction on the periphery of a large area surrounding the point of attack to ensure that their getaway route would not be obstructed.

They picked a particularly narrow street in which trucks were regularly parked on both sides. A large van pulled out suddenly and crushed the wing of the Ambassador's car. The chauffeur got out to take particulars of the 'accident'. This was a mistake, because it not only enabled the kidnappers to strike him down but also to get into the car through his door which was normally, of course, locked while the car was on the move. Meanwhile, other terrorists standing around in the area produced guns and opened fire, wounding two of the Ambassador's escorts, who were, by his decision, unarmed. Four terrorists got into the car and administered a 'pistol whipping' to the Ambassador as they drove away. The plan for blocking the access roads had worked, and the car had a clear run out into the suburbs, where he was transferred to a van and taken to a cellar which was to be his prison.

From the very first moment, while still in the car, Jackson made it clear that the British Government would not yield to any kind of pressure, whether his kidnappers killed him or not. Within a few hours, his wife was saying the same thing to the Uruguayan Foreign Ministry and the Foreign Office in London made a public statement to that effect. Throughout his captivity, they held to this, and no pressure was put on the Uruguayan Government to make concessions for his release.

There is no sure protection of an individual from kidnapping unless he never appears in public without a massive deployment of manpower, not only to protect his person, but also to block every possible escape route. In the Philippines in the early 1970s, it was not uncommon for leading politicians to have bodyguards forty strong. Such numbers could not possibly be provided for diplomats or business executives, even if it were known which of them were likely targets. An escort vehicle with three or four bodyguards is the most that is likely to be practical, and if the terrorists deploy, say, four vehicles and five teams of three or four men each they should have a very good chance of capturing their victim, even if he is in a locked and bullet-proofed car. The solution for prevention of kidnapping must therefore lie in intelligent variation of route and time, coupled with a highly efficient police framework with good communications, whereby police roadblocks under radio control can be deployed on every exit route within a few minutes. This is very expensive both in manpower and in police training, but such a framework is desirable in any case for dealing with normal crime and most police forces aim to get as close to it as they can. By far the most promising answer is where there is a high degree of police/public co-operation. Otherwise, the only guarantee of safety is for a man under particular threat to live within the protected walls of his place of work, or for a group of such men to live with their families in a defended compound and move to work in large escorted convoys.

In practice, kidnappings are bound to occur, but the number of kidnap victims who are killed is relatively small. One reason for this is that, once dead, the victim is of no further bargaining value to the kidnappers. Moreover, killing a hostage causes a particular revulsion of public opinion. Shortly before Sir Geoffrey Jackson's kidnapping, the Tupamaros had kidnapped and killed an American police adviser, Dan Mitrione. Despite the fact that he was a C.I.A. man who instructed the Uruguayan police in interrogation methods, his murder caused a massive alienation of public opinion from the Tupamaros. Till then, they had been regarded as a rather daring young band of Robin Hoods, who robbed the rich to help the poor, and who kidnapped people and released them just to show their infallibility. The murder of Mitrione, who had nine children, put an end to that image.

Sir Geoffrey Jackson's endurance of his ordeal has become a classic in the history of terrorism. Despite the calculated destruction of his dignity in the sordid conditions of a cellar sometimes ankle-deep in sewage, he reminded them throughout that he was the British Ambassador and would make no comments that were not proper for an Ambassador to make. He believes that by thus 'institutionalizing' himself he was able to maintain his pride and resistance better than if he had thought of himself purely as an individual. He never lost his sense of humour, and this enabled him to establish a relationship with quite a number of those who guarded him. After eight months, it was the Tupamaros who were on the defensive; they knew that they would lose heavily and gain nothing if they killed him but, with none of their demands met, they could not release him without loss of face.

Eventually, a large-scale escape from gaol by 106 Tupamaro prisoners gave them the pretext they needed to let him go. By holding out, he and the two Governments had destroyed the legend of Tupamaro infallibility completely. In the general election shortly after his release, the *Frente Amplio*, which gave political support to the Tupamaros, lost more than half the votes which public opinion polls had led it to expect before the kidnapping, and a government was returned with a clear mandate to end terrorism. It has done so with a ruthlessness and sacrifice of civil liberties harsh even by Latin American standards—a tragedy in what has traditionally been one of the most liberal countries in Latin America. The only crumb of comfort for such Tupamaros as survive in hiding is that, by provoking repression, they may have created a society sufficiently brittle to be more vulnerable in years to come than its liberal predecessor.

Sir Geoffrey Jackson showed how a hostage can establish a relationship with his captors in the most unpromising circumstances. Since then, much more has been learned about this, especially in the years 1974 and 1975. In August of 1974, two bank robbers held four hostages in the vault of a bank in Stockholm. The police, besieging the vault, inserted a microphone and recorded every word spoken between the criminals and their hostages; advised by a psychologist, they were able to strike (using tear gas) at a moment when they were confident that the gunmen would surrender without killing their captives, with whom they had by then built up a remarkable relationship. The hostages, in fact, insisted that the gunmen should be allowed to leave first as they feared that the police would shoot them if they were left behind in the vault. Detailed study of the tape recording taught psychologists many lessons which they were able to apply in subsequent sieges.

The police of the Republic of Ireland put this knowledge to good use during the siege by two I.R.A. terrorists holding a Dutch industrialist, Dr. Herrema, for thirty-one days in October and November 1975. Unlike the Swedish bank robbers, at least one of the terrorists, Marion Coyle, was said by Dr. Herrema to have spoken no single word to him for the whole of the time they were together. Dr. Herrema himself, however, said on the day of his release that he had felt a fatherly feeling towards them as they were about the same age as his own son, and the other kidnapper, Eddie Gallagher, was human enough at the end at least to give him the bullet from the gun which had been kept pointed at him so often during the previous month. The icy hostility of his female companion, however, suggests that political fanatics retain fewer vestiges of humanity than normal criminals.

This had been again demonstrated a few weeks earlier when criminals held the staff of the Spaghetti House Restaurant at gunpoint in the basement. At least one of the victims now visits his captor in prison. By contrast, the four I.R.A. men who held Mr. and Mrs. Matthews hostage for five days in Balcombe Street in December 1975 appear to have shown no warmth at all, though they did surrender without killing them.

The sum of all this experience should be of substantial value in dealing with future kidnappings though, presumably, political terrorist groups will attempt to indoctrinate their members further against being weakened in their resolve by the revival of their humanity.

Hi-jacking of aircraft is another field in which remarkable progress has been made since 1972. This progress was most dramatic in the U.S.A. During the previous five years (1968–72) nearly half the world's hi-jackings had been in aircraft taking off from U.S. airports. In 1971, of sixty-one hi-jack attempts worldwide, twenty-nine were from U.S. airports, and the figures for 1972 were another twenty-nine out of sixty-four. On 5th January 1973, a new system of protection against hi-jacking was introduced at all U.S. airports, and in the subsequent four years (January 1973–December 1976) there were only four hi-jack attempts on flights originating in the U.S.A., and all of these failed.

The new measures were simple but comprehensive, comprising a 100 per cent search of every passenger and every piece of baggage, hand or hold, on every flight at every U.S. airport. Up till then, searches had been largely confined to people who fell within a 'profile', prepared by psychologists—based on such assumptions as that all hi-jackers thus far had been aged between sixteen and sixty-five and had bought a single ticket for cash. Surprisingly, only two per cent fell within this profile and other profiles narrowed the number to half of one per cent. Only these were searched. Thereafter, protection relied upon 'sky marshals' in the aircraft. These measures reduced the success rate of hi-jackings from seventy-seven to eighty-seven per cent in 1968–70 to forty-four per cent in 1971 and forty-one per cent in 1972. Nevertheless, the rate was still too high.

The new measures were introduced by Lieutenant-General Benjamin O. Davis, Jr., who had been made responsible by the President for combatting hi-jacking two years earlier. Experience had convinced him that selective searching was inadequate, and that sky marshals were of little use once a hi-jacker had got on board the aircraft with a gun or grenade in his possession. The answer was a 100 per cent search at the boarding gates.

Davis realized that this would not work without the full co-operation of the airlines and airport authorities, and that this in turn depended on the search procedures being faster than the procedures for checking in at the ticket counter and then, after search, at the boarding lobby. If ever a queue was allowed to build up at the search barrier, harassed officials would be tempted to let the passengers through without proper search but, if the queues were always at the ticket counter and the boarding lobby, there would be no such temptation. This required a massive deployment of security men and search equipment. Davis was again shrewd in deciding that this should be paid for by the airport authorities, and only monitored by the F.B.I. This meant, in effect, that the airports had to recover the cost from the passengers on the air tickets, which was fair enough as it was the passengers who were being protected.

During the first year (1973) 150 million passengers were searched at 531 airports in the U.S.A. Of these, 300 declined the search and so were turned away. Another 3,200 were arrested, carrying between them 2,000 guns and 3,500 lb. of high explosives. The result—four attempts in four years, all unsuccessful —speaks for itself.

This is a good example of the potential of really efficient routine police work, coupled with a small degree of sacrifice in personal liberty, to which few passengers now object. The cost, however, in money and manpower, is a measure of the price society has to pay for its terrorists—diversion of resources which could otherwise be used for alleviating suffering and distress, or for fighting normal crime.

4*

9 The price to pay

What price should a community be prepared to pay in terms of sacrifice of civil liberties to defeat terrorism? This depends on the climate of public opinion. The government's dilemma in deciding how far to go with anti-terrorist measures has much in common with its dilemma in deciding how far to stand firm in the face of terrorist blackmail—which was discussed in Chapter 1. In both cases, the government should go only so far as it can carry public opinion with it. Otherwise, if it seems to its own public to be over-reacting or showing excessive ruthlessness, it may drive more people into joining the very small number who have sympathy for the terrorists and who are willing to give them shelter. The government's freedom of action therefore depends a great deal on the covering of events in the mass media—especially on television.

There have been occasions on which the media have been able to co-operate with the police in keeping a kidnapping secret in order to facilitate the release of the victim and the arrest of the kidnappers. This, however, is rarely possible in a free society. It would certainly not have been possible in any of the examples quoted so far for, as soon as anyone other than those immediately concerned is aware of the situation, there will be a public demand for news. This will be met by an urgent competition amongst the media for pictures and reports of the action, and will be further fed by the desire of the terrorists for publicity, which may be the main aim, or even the only aim, of their operation.

In addition to giving them the publicity they seek, coverage in the media helps international terrorist movements in several ways: it spreads ideas and techniques to fraternal groups in other countries; and, locally, it may give the terrorists an insight into police plans (especially in a siege situation) of which they might otherwise be unaware.

On the other hand, because the overwhelming majority of the public are hostile to acts of terrorism, the media will tend to present news of the terrorists in an unsympathetic light, and this will encourage the public to support the police, as well as giving them a better understanding of how they can best help them.

News can be suppressed only in totalitarian societies, such as Russia or China, where no news is published other than that which the government thinks it good for the people to know. This certainly has the effect of cutting terrorism in these countries to virtually nothing chiefly because, with no publicity, the incentive for political violence is largely removed, but also because the government action taken against it, however ruthless, does not become known to the public and cannot therefore alienate them. The price of stifling terrorism in this way, however, is a very heavy one. Once a government assumes total control of news, it is likely to use this power to suppress all kinds of dissent, and both Hitler and Stalin were able to conduct the most brutal State terror with no public awareness of it at all. In the long run, this not only makes for a more unpleasant society, but also a society more brittle and vulnerable to internal explosion.

The television camera is therefore something which a free society has to live with. In the context of political violence, it can be compared to a weapon lying in the street, which either side can pick up and use. Indeed, it is more powerful than any other weapon. Revolutionaries, whether violent or not, study its use incessantly, and become expert at extracting the maximum dividends from it. Governments and their security forces, and members of the public who wish to help them, are less expert, but they are learning by experience. In Northern Ireland, the Government's decision in 1971 to allow soldiers of any rank to speak directly into the microphone in front of the camera if they wished has paid tremendous dividends. Until then, only official spokesmen—officers, officials and politicians—and members of the public (who might be sympathetic or otherwise) were able to speak. Once the junior N.C.O. and soldier began to speak, even if occasionally he scored an 'own goal', the effect on public opinion, both in Britain and in Ireland, was dramatic. The Corporal came through to the living-room on the television screen far more effectively than the Colonel or the General or the Minister, and completely refuted the image of 'fascist pigs' on the street, which their enemies endeavoured to present. The result has been overwhelming British public support for the soldiers.

It is more difficult for this principle to be applied to the police, because the constable involved may have to prepare the prosecution and, if he has spoken publicly on television, it may be possible for defence lawyers to upset a conviction. Nevertheless, the use of the media in the Balcombe Street siege in London in December 1975 enormously enhanced the reputation of the Metropolitan Police, and the public desire to give them active support against the terrorists.

How big a price is it worth paying to defeat terrorism? The price of total government control of the media is clearly too high except in time of war and for a strictly limited period even then. But how far should we be prepared to sacrifice other civil liberties?

Routine police work, if effective enough, can keep the curtailment of civil liberties to a minimum, as has been proved in the measures taken against hi-jacking. Apart from the cost in money and manpower, effective police work against terrorism depends above all on intelligence, and intelligence depends on public co-operation. There have been some good examples of this in Britain. Of the eleven terrorists who attempted to blow up Scotland Yard and the Old Bailey in March 1973, ten were arrested and convicted. The majority of those responsible for the M62 coach bomb, which killed twelve people in February 1974, and for the Guildford and Woolwich pub bombs which killed five people later in the year, are now in prison. All those immediately concerned in placing the bombs which killed twenty-one people in pubs in Birmingham on 21st November 1974 were arrested within a few hours and have been subsequently convicted. All of these suggest a high standard of police intelligence and of quick response based upon it. The same applies to the operation which led to the capture of the gang which was attempting to escape from pursuit by the police when it kidnapped Mr. and Mrs. Matthews in Balcombe Street.

After the Birmingham bombs, the Government introduced the Prevention of Terrorism (Temporary Provisions) Act of 1974. This made it an offence to belong to the I.R.A. or to solicit or provide it with funds, or to give it propaganda support. It also increased the power of the police to hold for investigation those suspected of using or supporting terrorism, and for demanding evidence of identity at air and sea ports. The Act did not, however, change the rules for investigation or evidence; nor did it introduce identity cards or lodging registration; nor, despite a massive public demand for it, did it introduce capital punishment.

A public opinion poll late in 1975 showed that eighty-eight per cent of the British public were in favour of the death penalty for terrorist offences. Nevertheless, it was rejected in the House of Commons. This rejection was based on the opinion that the death penalty would reduce rather than increase the number of convictions for a number of reasons. Firstly, because terrorists on the run would be more likely to find people willing to give them shelter. Secondly, because witnesses would be less ready to give evidence if that evidence could send a prisoner, especially a young man or a girl, to their death. Thirdly, because juries would be less likely to convict, for the same reason—this being further compounded by the fact that juries sending a man to his death would clearly have to reach a unanimous verdict, and defence lawyers have now become skilled at objecting to juries until they can be sure that the jury will contain at least some who will vote for acquittal under any circumstances; on a capital charge one would be enough. And finally, because terrorists would deliberately use young boys and girls to do the actual killing, knowing that they would not be subject to the death penalty. Almost all criminologists agree that the real deterrent to a murderer is not the penalty but the likelihood of conviction, and if the conviction rate were reduced, the number of killings would increase.

The Prevention of Terrorism Act of 1974 was necessary for two reasons: firstly, to enable the police to protect the public and secure more convictions; and secondly because, if no action had been taken after the Birmingham bombs, there was a risk of an infuriated public taking the law into its own hands. If a substantial number of people become exasperated with the inability of the police to protect them from violence, and with the inadequacy of the processes of law in securing arrests and convictions, there is a real danger of a violent backlash. This has been seen repeatedly in Northern Ireland. In Birmingham, after the bombs, a number of Irishmen's homes and shops were attacked and burned, despite urgent pleas by the Prime Minister, and by local and religious leaders of all communities, not to take it out on the ordinary Irish who were just as revolted by the bombing as anyone else. Had this backlash gained momentum, it would have driven at least some of the Irish community into turning to the I.R.A. to organize some defence for them, and it could have irrevocably damaged the relationship between the one and a half million Irishmen living in Britain and the rest of the community. Vigilante groups would have sprouted on both sides, leading to public persecution of Irishmen on the streets, and worse, to a persecution like that of the Jews in Nazi Germany.

In some countries, the police themselves have become exasperated with the inadequacy of the law, and with their inability to secure convictions in the courts. The first symptom of this exasperation is seen when the police start planting or rigging evidence, or using illegal methods of interrogation. The next stage is for the police themselves to start beating people up or even killing them rather than arresting them. The final stage is for the police to make deals with rival political gangs or with criminal gangs, whereby those gangs agree to 'eliminate' suspected terrorists or supporters in exchange for the police allowing them latitude for their own activities. This is the beginning of the end for democracy, as has been seen in a number of Latin American countries.

If terrorism reaches such a scale as to be beyond the control of the police, even backed by the most stringent emergency legislation, how then should society react? The army forms the ultimate defence of the state against internal destruction. Most countries, however also have a 'Third Force', or several such forces, between the police and the army, to deal with internal security. The French C.R.S. (Compagnies Républicaines de Sécurité) was formed specifically to avoid the army being called out in such circumstances, because of the long record of military intervention in French politics. Holland and Italy also have such forces, and West Germany formed a special anti-terrorist force, initially about 240 strong, as a result of the Palestinian terrorist attacks at Munich and elsewhere and the activities of their own Baader-Meinhof gang.

In Britain, there exists no organization between the army and

the police to deal with either riots or terrorist attacks, and policemen themselves are unarmed unless specifically detailed to deal
with armed criminals or terrorists. To date, this has worked well,
especially in the Public Order role. Only nine people have been
killed in riots or strikes in England, Scotland and Wales since
1842, and none at all since 1919, until a demonstrator was killed
in Red Lion Square in 1974. Apart from traffic accidents, no one
has been killed in an industrial dispute since 1911, in fighting
either between strikers and police or strikers and blacklegs. The
army has not been called out in a Public Order role in mainland
Britain since 1919—surely a world record.

The army has regularly been deployed to assist the police in a
Public Security role, that is, in defence against armed attack,
whether with bombs or guns. Defence against armed attack is the
normal role of an army, whether the attack is by an enemy landing
on the beaches, or by parachutists, or by infiltrators, and is
accepted without demur by the public. This was clearly demonstrated when the army deployed at Heathrow Airport against
possible attack by Palestinian terrorists with surface-to-air
missiles in 1975. Although deployed, however, British troops have
not opened fire in England, Scotland or Wales since 1919.

In what circumstances should the police call upon the army for
assistance in Public Security? Where the attack or threat can be
adequately dealt with by a small number of individual marksmen,
this is best left to the police. (There are some who think that the
appearance on television of policemen with guns in the Balcombe
Street siege created a dangerous and false impression of an
armed police force, but on balance there is no doubt that the siege
brought them credit and public confidence.) Soldiers should be
called in when it seems likely that the attack may lead to a tactical
battle involving fire and movement; that is, when two or more
widely separated units of armed men have to operate as a team,
one group giving covering fire, while others close with the enemy
from a different direction. The British police are neither equipped
nor trained for such a role, and it is better that they should not be.
That is why Sir Robert Mark had no hesitation in calling on the
army to meet the threat at Heathrow.

Britain does not need a 'Third Force' because there is nothing
it could do which either the police (with marksmen) or the army

(with infantry platoons or the S.A.S.) could not do better. The police already have the Special Patrol Group (S.P.G.) consisting of about 200 carefully selected police constables, trained to act as marksmen if needed. For anything beyond the power of the police, the army is already well trained and enjoys an unprecedented degree of public confidence in England as a result of the television coverage of soldiers showing creditable restraint in the face of attack and provocation in Northern Ireland.

If terrorist attacks in England were to become so frequent that it was necessary to have tactical units permanently standing by in several parts of the country, these could best be found either by earmarking army units for this purpose, or by extending the size, training and functions of the S.P.G. In the latter case, it would be possible to train selected squads of policemen to fight like infantry platoons, but it would in that case be wise to second constables to that duty for a limited period after which they would return to normal police duties. Otherwise, there would be a risk of a rather different type of man emerging in police uniform, and creating a rather different image. On the whole, it will be better to leave such tasks to the army, as now.

In any case, all units in an internal security role in England, whether policemen or soldiers, should be under the control of the senior police officer responsible for law and order in the area. This was certainly the case at Heathrow, where the soldiers were under the tactical command of an army Lieutenant-Colonel or Major, but he was in turn responsible to the Metropolitan Police Commander, and not through any military channel to the Ministry of Defence.

This, however, depends on a continuing climate of general public support for the police. If, in some British city, this climate were to break down, only then would it be necessary for the army to take responsibility. This happened in Northern Ireland in 1969 when, for historical as well as for immediate reasons, large sections of the public did not accept the right of the Stormont Government to govern, nor the validity of its laws, nor the right of the Royal Ulster Constabulary to enforce those laws—and this applied particularly in the very areas in which the violence was occurring. In these circumstances, there was no alternative but for the British Army to take responsibility for law and order.

There is no city in Britain itself, however, where police/public relations are ever likely to break down to this extent.

Generally, the more the ordinary police constable is seen defending the public against terrorism the better. The terrorist attacks of the past three years have done much for the public image of the police. Whenever a suspicious suitcase, parked car or shopping bag is reported, the public knows that it is a policeman who is first on the scene, to risk his life by inspecting it before deciding what to do. When shooting or explosions are heard, the unarmed policeman turns towards it and tries to block the escape of the gunmen or bomber while ordinary citizens take cover. When four heavily armed gunmen barricaded themselves in the Matthews' flat in Balcombe Street, it was the police who closed and faced them at point-blank range until they surrendered.

These incidents have reinforced the relationship which has existed between the police and the public in Britain for over a century. This relationship was quantified in a remarkable study by Dr. William Belson, Head of the Survey Research Centre of the London School of Economics, published under the title of *The Public and The Police* by Harper & Row in 1975. In a three-year operation which dwarfed any normal public opinion poll, a large sample of the London public, both adults and teenagers, was questioned in depth. The most significant results were summarized in a table listing the degree to which the respondent 'respected', 'trusted', 'liked' and was 'satisfied with' the Metropolitan Police. Such qualifications as 'a lot', 'quite a lot', 'not very much', etc. were recorded. Amongst adults ninety-eight per cent 'respected' the police, seventy-three per cent of them 'a lot'. Ninety per cent 'trusted' the police, thirty per cent of them 'completely'. Ninety-three per cent 'liked' the police, thirty-one per cent 'very much'. Ninety-six per cent were 'satisfied' with the police, sixty-one per cent of them 'very satisfied'.

Teenagers (aged thirteen to twenty) gave surprisingly similar answers. Ninety-four per cent 'respected' the police, eighty-three per cent 'trusted' them and eighty-five per cent 'liked' them. Dr. Belson did not ask the teenagers whether they were 'satisfied' with the police, but asked them instead whether they were 'scared' of them. Forty-five per cent were 'not at all scared', forty-one per cent 'just a bit', twelve per cent 'fairly' and two per cent 'very scared'. (One is tempted to wonder what this two per cent had been up to!)

With support like this, the police need not doubt that the public want to help them, and that in the face of terrorist attack this support is almost universal. The public can help in three ways: firstly, by not doing anything, even inadvertently, to help the terrorists; secondly by co-operating with the police when measures involving some inconvenience have to be imposed; and thirdly, by providing information. An alert public can save lives, like the ticket collector and station manager who spotted and removed a 20 lb. bomb in Oxford Circus Underground Station, timed to go off in the rush hour, on 13th February 1976. They can also be the eyes and ears of the police Special Branch, drawing attention to suspicious behaviour, suspicious packages, suspicious arrivals and departures, suspicious cars, and suspicious houses, garages, workshops or warehouses which they think might be in use as 'safe houses' from which the terrorists are operating or plan to operate. Such reports will result in no more than investigation, and if the investigation proves negative, nothing is lost but police manhours. When searching for a needle in a haystack, however, any clue which helps Special Branch to look in the right direction puts them on the road to success.

Guerrilla warfare and terrorism have come to stay. Political violence may be justified in some countries, and may have been justified in Britain in the past, but is certainly not justified in Britain today. Even in countries where moral justification might be claimed for it, it is in fact unlikely to pay, especially in the long term.

Intervention in internal conflict has become the prevalent modern method of making war. Terrorism has become international also in another respect, in that terrorist groups conduct operations in foreign countries with which they have no quarrel, but can provide a useful platform for 'armed propaganda'.

Most internal conflict, however, is aimed to destroy a form of society which the majority of people have chosen, when the terrorists find that they cannot persuade people to alter this choice by peaceful means. Most terrorists, though not all, are motivated by either anarchist or Marxist aims. The anarchist wishes to destroy the rule of law and release the community back into the jungle of unrestrained individual freedom. The Marxist aims to substitute his own rule of law by advancing civilization to the regimented state of the ant heap, of which he is on top. Since most people want neither of these things, society has a right to protect itself against them, answering force with force. If the people become exasperated, however, they may place power in the hands of an authoritarian regime which will regiment them into an alternative ant heap which is almost indistinguishable from the Marxist one.

Democratically elected governments which are subject to free elections, maintain free speech and freedom of the press and try to accommodate non-violent dissent, therefore face a constant dilemma. If they do not stand firm enough, this may bring about that exasperation which will sweep away these freedoms. If, however, they themselves over-react and stifle dissent, this will not only poison their society, but will make it more brittle and vulnerable to attack.

The mass media can play a decisive role. Terrorists know this, and become expert at exploiting the media to publicize their cause and to spread the effect of their terror. If they are to survive this kind of attack, the governments, security forces and people of democratic societies must also understand how the media can be of value to them. Since reporters, editors and producers thrive on the numbers of readers and viewers they can attract, their coverage will have a strong incentive to be hostile to the terrorists since the overwhelming majority of the public are hostile to them. If the media betray or hamper the police, or cause unnecessary loss of life, the public will not lightly forgive them. They should therefore be treated, not as enemies, but as friends and allies, and very powerful ones they can be.

It is appropriate to end with a story which illustrates many aspects of terrorist warfare. It was told by a fireman who was one of the first on the scene at one of the pubs destroyed by I.R.A. bombs in Birmingham on 21st November 1974. Only firemen, doctors and ambulance men were being allowed in. In the beam of his torch, amongst the shambles, the fireman saw a torso from which all the clothing had been blown away. It had neither arms nor legs, and where the head had been there was a spongy, bloody mass. A few minutes earlier it had been a young man who had just collected his pay packet and had taken his girl for a drink. The torso was not only wriggling; it was also screaming, through the bloody mass above its neck. The fireman wanted to call in the colour television cameras to photograph it and transmit it straight into the living-rooms of a horrified public, to bring home to them just what terrorism meant.

The next few days provided the fireman with the answer to his suggestion. He was called out three times to extinguish fires at the home of an Irishman who had been in detention and had painted the Long Kesh emblem on his wall, which was too much for his neighbours. It is fair to suppose that, had they seen the wriggling screaming torso on their television screens, the homes of many other Irishmen wholly unconnected with the I.R.A. would also have been set on fire. The fury of the backlash, already at explosion point, might have been uncontrollable.

The raw material of terrorism is flesh and blood; its effect is fear and fury, both of which can be fanned by the media and which can, if uncontrolled, do more damage to society than the terrorists themselves. So can over-reaction or repression, which it is one of the aims of the terrorists to provoke. These things can best be avoided by public awareness of the real aims of the terrorists, of how they try to achieve them, and of how they can be prevented from doing so with minimum damage to the society they are attacking.

Bibliography

ARENDT, Hannah, *On Violence*. London, Penguin, 1970

ASHBY, E. and ANDERSON, M., *The Rise of the Student Estate in Britain*. London, Macmillan, 1970

ASPREY, Robert, *War in the Shadows*. New York, Doubleday, 1975

BELSON, William, *The Public and the Police*. London, Harper and Row, 1975

BOULTON, David, *The UVF 1966–73*. Dublin, Torc Books, 1973

BOULTON, David, *The Making of Tania Hearst*. London, New English Library, 1975

BOWDEN, Tom, *The Men in the Middle—The UK Police*. London, Institute for the Study of Conflict, 1976

BOWYER BELL, J., *Transnational Terror*. Washington, AEI Hoover Policy Studies, 1975

BOYLE, K. et al., *Law and the State: The Case of Northern Ireland*. London, Martin Robertson, 1975

BRINTON, Crane, *The Anatomy of Revolution*. New York, Vintage, 1957

BROWNE, Malcolm, *The New Face of War*. London, Cassell, 1966

BURNS, Alan, *The Angry Brigade*. London, Quartet, 1973

BURTON, Anthony, *Urban Terrorism*. London, Leo Cooper, 1975

CANTOR, Norman, *The Age of Protest*. London, Allen and Unwin, 1970

CARR, Gordon, *The Angry Brigade*. London, Gollancz, 1975

CLUTTERBUCK, Richard, *Living with Terrorism*. London, Faber and Faber, 1975

CLUTTERBUCK, Richard, *Riot and Revolution in Singapore and Malaya*. London, Faber and Faber, 1973

CLYNE, Peter, *An Anatomy of Skyjacking*. London, Abelard-Schuman, 1973

CROZIER, Brian, ed., *Annual of Power and Conflict*. London, Institute for the Study of Conflict, 1976

DEBRAY, Régis, *Revolution in the Revolution?* London, Penguin, 1968

DILLON, M. and LEHANE, D., *Political Murder in Northern Ireland.* London, Penguin, 1973

ELLIOTT BATEMAN, M. *et al.*, *Revolt to Revolution.* Manchester University Press, 1974

FALL, Bernard, *Street Without Joy: Insurgency in Indo-China 1946-63.* London, Pall Mall, 1964

FALL, Bernard, *The Two Vietnams.* London, Pall Mall, 1963

FANON, Frantz, *The Wretched of the Earth.* London, Penguin, 1967

GALVIN, John, *The Minute Men.* New York, Hawthorn, 1967

GELLNER, John, *Bayonets in the Streets.* Canada, Collier Macmillan, 1974

GIBSON, Brian, *The Birmingham Bombs.* London, Barry Rose, 1976

GILBERT, Martin, *The Arab–Israeli Conflict: Its History in Maps.* London, Weidenfeld and Nicolson, 1974

GIRLING, J. L. S., *People's War.* London, Allen and Unwin, 1969

GOODE, Stephen, *Affluent Revolutionaries.* New York, New Viewpoint, 1974

GURR, T. R., *Why Men Rebel.* Princeton University Press, 1970

HANNING, Hugh, *The Peaceful Use of Military Forces.* New York, Praeger, 1967

HAN SUYIN, *And The Rain My Drink.* London, Cape, 1956

HODGES, D. C., ed., *Philosophy of the Urban Guerrilla: The Revolutionary Writings of Abraham Guillen.* New York, Morrow, 1973

JACKSON, Geoffrey, *People's Prison.* London, Faber and Faber, 1973

JANKE, Peter and PRICE, D. L., *Ulster: Coercion and Consensus.* London, Institute for the Study of Conflict, 1974

KITSON, Frank, *Bunch of Five.* London, Faber and Faber, 1977

KITSON, Frank, *Low Intensity Operations.* London, Faber and Faber, 1971

LAFFIN, John, *Fedayeen: The Arab Israeli Dilemma.* London, Cassell, 1973

LAQUEUR, Walter, *The Road to War.* London, Penguin, 1969

LAQUEUR, Walter, *Guerrilla.* London, Weidenfeld and Nicolson, 1976

LAWRENCE, T. E., *The Seven Pillars of Wisdom*. London, Cape, 1973

MACFARLANE, Leslie, *Violence and the State*. London, Nelson, 1974

MCKNIGHT, Gerald, *The Mind of the Terrorist*. London, Michael Joseph, 1974

MAGEE, John, *Northern Ireland: Crisis and Conflict*. London, Routledge and Kegan Paul, 1974

MARIGHELA, Carlos, *For the Liberation of Brazil*. London, Penguin, 1971

PARRY, Albert, *Terrorism: from Robespierre to Arafat*. New York, Vanguard, 1976

PHILLIPS, David, *Skyjack*. London, Harrap, 1973

PRICE, D. L., *Jordan and Palestinians: The PLO's Prospects*. London, Institute for the Study of Conflict, 1975

PRIESTLAND, Gerald, *The Future of Violence*. London, Hamish Hamilton, 1974

PYE, Lucian, *Guerrilla Communism in Malaya*. Princeton University Press, 1956

SHORT, Anthony, *The Communist Insurrection in Malaya, 1948–60*. London, Frederick Muller, 1957

SMITH, Colin, *Carlos: Portrait of a Terrorist*. London, André Deutsch, 1976

STYLES, George, *Bombs Have No Pity*. London, Luscombe, 1975

TABER, Robert, *The War of the Flea*. London, Paladin, 1970

THOMPSON, Sir Robert, *Defeating Communist Insurgency*. London, Chatto and Windus, 1966

THOMPSON, Sir Robert, *No Exit from Vietnam*. London, Chatto and Windus, 1969

THOMPSON, Sir Robert, *Peace is Not at Hand*. London, Chatto and Windus, 1974

VAN DER HAAG, E., *Political Violence and Disobedience*. New York, Harper and Row, 1972

WILKINSON, Paul, *Political Terrorism*. London, Macmillan, 1974

WILKINSON, Paul, *Terrorism versus Liberal Democracy: The Problem of Response*. London, Institute for the Study of Conflict, 1976

Index